Kicking the **HELL** Out of mice

While Elephants Are Waltzing Out The Back Door

Joseph T. Di Bene

ISBN: 1439268533
ISBN-13: 9781439268537

Table of Contents

Acknowledgements

My sincere thanks to my daughter Jamie for her encouragement; she did a yeoman's job of editing. I will never know how she found time with her teaching schedule and raising her family. Also, I would like to thank my son Ted for his encouragement, who on many occasions prodded me to get on with finishing this book.

My special thanks to my friend and colleague Barry Hanks. I could always depend on his broad understanding of the subject mater and his raising a red flag when something I wrote did not make sense.

Most of all, my thanks to the truly bad managers and executives who dotted my career. They provided me with deep sense of reality that allowed me to recognize and confront the many forms of incompetent, sinister, and blundering management. This insight was invaluable in my role as a troubleshooter and *"Company Doctor"* (One who fixes sick companies). Without this exposure to the real-live management drama, one would only have a textbook view of the incredibly complex and dark side of management, a limitation shared by more then a few so-called management experts.

CREDITS

This book would not have been possible if it were not for the inept, greedy, self-centered, political, and insincere CEO's and executives I have come in contact with during my career. Without these people I would never have come to understand the dark side of management. Thank you.

And

To the really great managers and the few real leaders I have known, I thank you for your courage and steadfast devotion to the simple but true elements of management. Sincerity, devotion, decisiveness, tenacity and intense dedication marked your path. Your way has not been easy, but looking back, the alternatives were unthinkable.

Something to Consider

To reach the management summits, you must pass through the eleven gates of hell. The passage is fraught with unspeakable perils and few rewards. Is it worth it? That question might be answered by considering the alternative of laboring forever in the bottomless pit of lower management.

Written By: Joseph T.

PREAMBLE

It is difficult to understand the incredible rate of business failures in the last twenty or so years. Few will agree on the exact statistics, but some say that approximately thirty-five percent of aspiring companies survive in first five years. The dilemma is that in this marvelous age of scientific enlightenment and unlimited access to endless data, we do not seem to learn from our mistakes. Yes, there are forces afoot that challenge the business world in new and unpredictable ways. However, the majority of reasons that today's companies are brought down is due to the most fundamental mistakes management can make.

The increasing rate of failure is alarming and shows no signs of abating. The investments in human and financial resources are being squandered at an alarming rate. To complicate maters, the world of management has taken on an air of increased complexity that far too often becomes the excuse for failure. In this book, I will do my best to show that the majority of the failures are preventable and less complex than we are led to believe, and that at the heart of most failures is the manager and the executive.

More then ever before, the business world is being invaded by management fads and wild theories on how to reinvent yourself, your environment and your company to become an overnight success. Nothing is as easy as some management experts are telling us. What is needed is a return to the fundamentals while acknowledging the need for innovation and creativity.

About This Book

There are doubtless many reasons to write a book. The most oblivious are: For profit, an ego trip, to gain status . . . and so on. This book, however, was written primarily to inform and to correct misconceptions, old and new, and to point the finger of blame for failure where it belongs.

The ideas, experiences and comments in the book are derived from the real world of founding and managing over fifteen companies in many of the free world countries. Also, my experience as a "Company Doctor" (fixing sick companies) has added to my cognizance and understanding of the business world in which I live. This book is not an exercise in theory or academic observations. Also, it is not based on statements from business leaders and would-be experts that sometimes pollute our minds with profound nonsense. Further, there are very few quotations that I feel worthy of passing on to you that would improve your impact on the business world.

Chapter I

Nothing stands out so clearly as a manager and or executive who consistently sweeps aside confusing inputs and obstacles to get right to the heart of the issues, and with precise focus, attacks the issues with determination and zeal.

And

Nothing is so frustrating as a manager or executive who squanders his and others' energies on immaterial, non-critical and self-serving issues.

WHAT IS KICKING THE HELL OUT OF MICE?

As the phrase suggests, it is working on trivial or low priority problems and issues and with incorrect priorities while the critical ones are ignored and often unrecognized. It is also about jumping all over small problems because the big ones are out of management's league.

Have you ever had the feeling that your company ship is sinking and your headed for certain failure? But, what is management doing? Are they frantically working to plug the hole in the ship's hull or are they having meetings discussing the color for a new company logo?

Or

> The Vendors are not being paid and the new bank loan is not complete, but the Vice President of Finance spends most of his time checking expense reports for the smallest error.

Or

> The company launches a new austerity program freezing salaries and bonuses and at the same time buys a fleet of new company cars for the executives.

Or

> The CEO has hired an expensive consultant team to lower cost. They make their recommendations based on interviews with the management staff that has made the same recommendations to the CEO – many times.

Or

> Your boss likes to badger the troops by frequently calling meetings to preach how he or she has personally achieved success.

Or

> Management is busily cranking out status reports, statistics and long-range projections for the next five years, but has badly missed shipments for three months in a row.

Or

> The boss has the office supplies located so he can see who gets pencils, writing pads and paperclips, but fly's first class and checks into the best hotel suites wherever he goes on company business.

Or

> Your boss calls a meeting every time his boss chews him out, and the message is
>
> > "You people better shape up"

Or

> The accounting department issues a forty page report on what happened the last quarter but the operations department cannot get basic information about what happened last week or last month.

Or

> Committees are formed to deal with long-term strategy while daily problems are mostly ignored by management.

TO SEE THE PRIORITIES IS TO KNOW

A management gift is to be able to see the real issues and the path to resolution. Not every manager or executive has that ability, but you can see it in the effective manager and in real leaders. The absence of it is equally obvious.

> **In my opinion, the ability to clearly see the essential priorities, through a hailstorm of distractions is the real management game.**

I remember a CEO that, more than any other executive I have ever known had that insight and a clear mental vision to see what was critical, and he seemed to' know instantly the priorities of the lesser issues. I remember the patience, or rather impatience, as he tried to drag his staff along to conclusions he saw long before we did. It was like we had to labor up the mountains of logic and down into the valleys while he jumped from mountain-top to mountain-top. The fact that he dragged us along at all was perhaps the most admirable element of his leadership. He could have, as many gifted leaders do, simply told us what he wanted us to do, and never mind the reasons.

He helped many of us start a learning process through thinking – something about which far too many managers and executives are seldom burdened.

TIME WORKS AGAINST SUCCESS

Kicking mice, or working on the wrong problems at the wrong times saps the company's energy and squanders time. Time is perhaps the most precious commodity to an enterprise. There is a rule, not scientific but usually correct, that says:

There is be barely enough time to do the right things, and then, only if they are done in the right order.

Companies often fail because they run out of time before they can do the right things. Small to medium and epically start-up companies are always racing against the clock. The financial clock is ticking, and the competition is racing to the next product win. More than ever before the market windows are closing faster than many companies can cope with. **Time** is the ruthless adversary.

The problem is that most managers and executives squander time like it could be replenished, which, of course, it cannot. Once spent, wasted or squandered, it is gone forever. The phrase, "to save time," is used freely by everyone, but we don't really save time, do we? Saving time would be akin to having a "time bank account" where you save up and you can withdraw some time when you run short. You might utilize time more efficiently or avoid wasting time but you can't save it.

There are several ways managers and executives waste time. The most common is working on the wrong problems, at the wrong time or doing immaterial and non-essential tasks by habit or by custom – that is **kicking mice**. Working on the wrong problems at the wrong time is often because those problems are what the manager is comfortable with and is capable of working with. Another reason is that his priority compass is defective or overridden by management crisis activities or the ambient distraction level is too high. They literally cannot see the forest through the trees; they do not know north from south.

TIME MANAGEMENT –THE SECRET OF SUCCESS?

I believe there are very few managers or executives that seriously practice time management, but their secretaries do it every day. There are far more secretaries that practice time management than do their bosses. In fact I would venture to say that most secretaries are excellent time managers of themselves and their bosses. After all, that is what they do all day long; they try to utilize the limited time to accommodate an inordinate and ever increasing workload with rapidly changing priorities.

My experience tells me that most managers have discretionary control of perhaps thirty to forty percent of their day, and then only if they aggressively protect it. What managers and executives desperately need is a good secretary that can protect that precious discretionary time so that his or her boss is available for most of the obligatory duties.

It is unrealistic to believe that most managers are capable of dissecting their day's activity into minutes and hours; they are too busy running in front of the bulls every day. Is this ineffective or bad management? No, but it is not efficient and sensible management ether.

A DAY IN THE LIFE OF A SUCCESSFUL MANAGER

To illustrate the point, let us follow an up-and-coming, successful executive as he plans out his day, laying in bed just before dawn.

> Joe Blunderbus (a fictitious name in a hypothetical scene) wakes up at 4:30 nearly every morning - except Sundays. Lying there in bed he lays out his day's work and ponders what he wants to accomplish. After going over his plan for the day he gets up and gets ready for work, still making refinements on his planned workday. This continues for another hour on his commute, until he reaches work.
>
> Settling back at his desk he reviews the list of meetings and scheduled phone calls he must do. His secretary has laid out the day with a few leftover scheduled meetings from yesterday and the day before. This is not exactly what he had been planning early that morning but his priorities are always changing. He asks the secretary to reschedule two meetings but the majority of the schedule looks acceptable. He would be happy if he

could work on some of the priorities he would like to address. Instead, most of his priorities are determined by someone else.

As the day progresses our manager hero has to cut short two meeting because of an unexpected staff meeting and an emergency oversees conference call. Just before lunch he is informed that an employee has been injured in a fork-lift accident. He spends thirty-five minutes in the nurse's office making sure that the employee is cared for. He decides to skip lunch and get some work done at his desk.

The afternoon is not looking that good for getting back on schedule, but he knows he can cut a few meetings short to make up some time. Just as he was getting ready for an employee meeting his secretary informs him of a crises marketing meeting involving the their third largest customer. After a 45-minute meeting, he once again heads for his office, but fate will once again intervene. The union shop steward corners him in the hallway and insists on discussing a grievance he has just received.

They find an empty conference room nearby and after thirty-five minutes, the shop steward is temporally pacified. and our manger, again, heads for his office. It is now almost four in the afternoon and the schedule is riddled with changes. Only four items were accomplished out of eleven. But, he has been working on problems throughout the entire day and making things happen.

Back in the office he gets a phone call from his wife who has had a very bad day. The carpet cleaner has bleached their oriental rug so it looks like a cheap imitation. She is furious and wants him to call the rug cleaning company to give them hell, and find out what they are going to do about it.

It's seven-thirty and Joe decides to pack it in and head for home when he notices that the last thing scheduled was a dinner meeting and a speech at the engineering graduating class at the local college. He should already be there.

As he heads out of the office, he realizes that he has not accomplished much of his planned schedule, but it has been a full day and a satisfying one, in fact, not a bad day at all.

And that is the problem with many of our hard working, successful executives – they thrive on activity – even on those less important and irrelevant tasks that should be done by someone else. They take on whatever the random forces have to throw at them, and in fact, they feel a real sense of accomplishment at the end of the day.

This is where a manager needs to take account of what he is accomplishing, not just what he is doing. And yet, it is nearly impossible for these warriors to step back from the battlefield and analyze the value of their daily effort. Unfortunately, it usually takes a cardiac event or something close to a nervous breakdown for them to start developing a perspective on the quality and the value of their work.

THANK GOD FOR SECRETARIES

There are too few managers and executive that give their secretary credit for their success in dealing with the real world. Yet, I wonder how effective these business warriors would be without their secretaries. A good secretary will design a protective barrier around his/her boss and stand at the gate defending that boss. They analyze data on a minute-by-minute basis and continually revise and adjust the time, appointments, priorities, and while doing their own work of typing, answering the phone, sending faxes, opening mail and analyzing E-mail, act as a receptionist, take dictation and meeting minutes, make copies and bring the boss coffee every thirty minutes. How do they do it?

WHO ARE THE MICE KICKERS?

Kicking the hell out of mice happens at every level of management. The problem is that Board of Directors, CEOs, Presidents and Senior Executives are often the guiltiest. When lower levels of management do it, they most likely learned it from upper management. Some managers and executives are vaguely aware that they are constantly being evaluated and ranked by their subordinates as well as their peers and superiors. They are examples for the subordinates to follow and sometimes emulate. When the boss is out kicking the hell out of mice, everyone is watching. If he or she gets away with it, or worse yet is rewarded, it becomes a lesson that is too well learned.

TYPES OF MICE KICKERS

There are several types of Mice Kickers that are easily identified. Here are some of them:

Bumbling McGee

This type can't seem to do anything right, like withdrawing a health perk and replacing it with two, much more valuable perks, but the employees were so confused by a poorly written announcement that they went on strike. He has good intentions but fails to take care of the details and that is why much of what he does turns out wrong.

Ignorant Bliss

This type is not aware of his shortcomings and lack of understanding of the job. He is in a world of his own. He believes that he is a good leader who is irreplace-able. When things go wrong he is convinced the fault belongs to someone else.

The Part Time Executive

This type is lazy and treats his job as an annoyance when there is work to do and when there are problems to solve. But, when there are celebrity functions or acco-lades to be given out, he is right there to receive them.

The Bull-Headed Loner

This type knows it all. He refuses to listen to any input that is counter to his own position. His direct reports have given up trying to tell him what is really going on - they no longer try.

The Lost Soul

This type is way over his head. He can't make decisions because he just doesn't know what to do. His staff is paralyzed and the company is slowly dying. No one can understand how he got the CEO job.

WHY DO THEY DO IT?

You can often tell how tall a manager or executive sits in the saddle by what problems he takes on and how he goes after the problems and issues. If he or she seems not to understand the *real* issues, and is off somewhere kicking the hell out of mice, that person is most likely operating within his or her own *Capability Envelope.* When real issues are left unattended and minor issues are given priority, it is often because that is what that manager of executive is capable of dealing with. It also happens that problems and issues that carry risks are often avoided by marginal management.

Your boss may not be a total nerd just because he or she works on the wrong problems or hesitates to act. The size or degree of difficulty of the problems or issues bosses tackle can be a measure of the skill and expertise they have to offer. Some managers and executives need only a small clue that they don't know. That's all it takes for them to start trying to find out. Others haven't got a clue that they do not know, and those are the lost ones.

THE CAPABILITY ENVELOPE

Your boss may need a job within his or her *Envelope of Capability*. But, as so often happens, they are rewarded, in spite of working on the wrong problems. In far too many companies, all he or she has to do is conform to the company culture, keep out of trouble, don't shake the trees, avoid provocative situations, keep a low profile on controversial issues and eagerly support the company line, what ever it happens to be, and a promotion is not far off. Now the problems begin to emerge. A promotion is great but now this person is exposed. He has been promoted beyond his envelope of capability. You have heard someone say: "I don't know what has happened to George since he was promoted, he was a great manager in his last job. He just can't get his act together. George can't get his act together.

WHAT GOES AROUND IS AROUND

Kicking the hell out of mice can become a contagious habit. If the bosses do it, you can be sure the troops will pick up on it. The longer it goes unchecked, the more difficult it is to address the real issues that face the company. Really tough issues are often avoided or shunned because it is much easier to tackle less difficult issues. It can become a way of company life, handed down from generations of bosses to their subordinates.

A BUILT-IN EXCUSE

A Silicon Valley company I worked with had a growing problem of falling behind the competition on new product releases, resolving quality and service complaints, and responding to customer ideas and requests. The CEO responded to the criticism by referring his critics to the company credo, which went something like:

> **"We will build our products to the most stringent quality and performances standards that will drive the industry."**

The gist of it was, "to be the best" meant the company was necessarily slower than the competition, but that superior products may take a little longer. The CEO was hiding behind the company credo by insisting slow was good because the company can benefit in other, more important ways. By this contrived logic he avoided the fact that his company was falling behind in many of the essential performance areas. These areas were laden with tough problems that the CEO was not capable of tackling. To make it worse, some of the areas in which they claimed to excel, were actually sub-par also.

THE REAL CHALLENGE

There are many ways to become sidetracked from the real issues and critical priorities. Kicking the hell out of mice is one way of expressing that problem.

> The real management challenge is to build a company of managers, executives and employees that have the insight to see the real issues and the skill and courage to go after them.

On the brighter side:

> "Kicking the hell out of mice does have one good effect; it can keep the Mice Kicking Boss busy doing something so that you can get on with kicking the hell out of elephants.

Chapter II

WHY COMPANIES FAIL

Except for very large meteors, 8.5 Richter Earthquakes and Germ Warfare, all company failures are most likely the responsibility of one or more managers, the President, the CEO, or the Board of Directors: And, oh yes, on occasion the CEO's wife.

INCOMPETENCE IS UNFORGIVABLE

It is not the *"Tried hard but didn't quite make it"* type of failure that is so tragic. What is disturbing is the unnecessary waste of the human effort because of bad or incompetent management. If you have worked hard and successfully for years, only to have the company fail because of management incompetence, you know the feeling of disappointment, despair and contempt for the people responsible. It is difficult to find company failure data that experts will agree upon, but one statistic says that something like 60% of companies fail in the first two years and 85% fail within five years. The reasons are varied but most informed sources agree that management is one of the key reasons for failure, and in my opinion it is the main reason. Some experts like to rank the reasons for failure, giving some reasons more weight then others, but it doesn't really get to the bottom of it. The truth is most companies fail because of more then one reason. These reasons encompass disciplines like finance, product planning, market performance, cost control, quality and manufacturing efficiency to name a few. Too often these are actually manifestations of the **real** reason, which is management incompetence - in one way or another. For example:

A young, Silicon Valley Company was growing at a fast rate due to a successful entry into a new electronics market. The staff were all college buddies of the CEO and founder, all of which had little management experience but were long on great attitude, drive and technical competence. When the company began the key Vice President positions were handed out by the CEO according to who had the time and wanted to take on the responsibility. As the company grew the need for competent decisions makers in key positions became more and more important. The Vice President of Finance had some experience in bookkeeping but no experience in raising money and corporate finance. His presentations to the banks and investors were amateurish and lacking important detail. The little money that was raised was too expensive.

The Vice president of Marketing was a natural salesman but had no idea how to study and analyze the market and the competitions strategy. The company ran out of money and failed to successfully launch new products, partly because of lack of development funds and partly because they didn't really know where the market was going. The failure here is oblivious; the founder and CEO failed to recognize the need for experienced people, in certain critical growth stages. Finance and

Marketing management failure to perform is a manifestation of the CEO's incompetence as he failed to hire a competent level of management, at the right time. The buck stops at the top.

This example seems too obvious to be believable, or that it may an exception. Not so, the majority of companies were once startups and so had to experience the limitations of founders and key people that, for one reason or another, did not develop as fast as their environment required. The difference between those developing companies that made it, and those that did not, was someone at the top that made the difficult decisions which allowed the company to continue to develop. Many times the right decision is to replace an old comrade or perhaps even someone who was part of the founding team. These can be tough decisions but the company's future could be at stake.

ALL THE WRONG REASONS

Some time ago I ran across a graduate paper on the failure of a well known Silicon Valley Electronics Company that I just happened to have consulted for during their **Hay-Day** - before their demise. I was amazed at the reasons given for the failure and the conclusions reached by the author. I was disappointed in the author's understanding of the reasons for failure, which pointed to market share, new product timing, competition, and complex finance issues. These reasons were actually manifestations of the real reasons, but they were not why the company failed. This company failed because of incompetent management in several key positions. I can't be too hard on the young author because seasoned and experienced managers, academics and executives often make the same mistake.

The paper was heavily supported by interviews from executives, a few having been with the company through the failing period. Others had been recently brought in to turn the company around. In both groups, the comments were heavily biased and reflected a strong self–promotional spin. The interviews had much to say about the technical reasons for failure but avoided the real reason, which was management incompetence. Executive interviews should be taken with grain of salt, because the interviewee's ego may be doing the talking.

A complex diagnosis of a failed company is not unusual and it is an example of some of the current management wisdom that can be wrong. These studious and multifarious theories can be misleading to people in search for real answers to real problems.

THE SOLUTION IS RIGHT THERE UNDER YOUR NOSE

If we are to fix anything, we must know the real reason or reasons for the problems.

The common practice is to dissect a company in deep trouble with complex and scientific scalpels that will invariably disclose complex and scientific reasons, which often calls for complex and drastic solutions. This is likely to be followed by harsh changes that can take the company further from the real issues and sensible solutions. Quite often the problem is right there in the open and the solution is as simple as replacing the CEO or one or more managers or executives.

LET'S LOOK FAILURE IN THE FACE

These are some of the *real* reasons why companies fail:

The simple truth is ***Most companies fail because they:***

Do not make good business decisions

Do not produce competitive and reliable products

Do not perform the basic accounting and finance functions

Do not understand their markets, employees, and customers

Do not have enough money

Do not provide for management transition

Do not hire competent people

Have lost their primary mission

Do not plan or follow and revise their plans

Do not develop strong and balanced business fundamentals

BUT, MOST IMPORTANTLY, COMPANIES FAIL BECAUSE THEY DO NOT HAVE CAPABLE MANAGEMENT

Anyone of the reasons for failure I have listed could destroy a company if badly managed. But, believe it or not, I have worked with companies that have mismanaged several of these crucial areas – at the same time. Gross incompetence is likely to infest several areas and disciplines, especially if the incompetence is at the top of the management pyramid.

DO NOT MAKE GOOD BUSINESS DECISIONS

Every day a company is called upon to make decisions, some of which are critical and the majority often appear to be routine. This is where many companies go astray. Managers and executives often delegate their responsibility to make decisions that appear to be below their status. Sometimes this is done because of a mistaken idea that managers need to delegate or they will not be perceived as promotable material. Delegation is not incorrect, although it is dangerous when done for the wrong reasons and by people that do not know how to do it. Even small decisions can have an impact. The message here is that there are few decisions that can be taken lightly. We will discuss delegation latter on.

DO NOT PRODUCE COMPETITIVE AND RELIABLE PRODUCTS OR SERVICES

The customers are usually the judge and jury in the determination of a company's fate. In the end, a superior product or service can make up for a lot of mistakes, but bad products or services leaves no reason for the existence of the company. Manufacturing and service companies have a great deal of competition. Inferior products or services have no place to hide. Customers are intense on finding a better product, better service and at competitive prices.

DO NOT PERFORM BASIC ACCOUNTING

A company without current and accurate accounting knowledge, systems and records is like a car with no brakes, careening down the side of a mountain to certain destruction. Measuring where you have been, what you did, and what you are doing, is the knowledge to know where to go, and often how to get there.

The first job of finance and accounting is to keep management out of the slammer, meaning the company must be operating inside the legal confines of whatever environment, authority, or jurisdiction is involved. The second responsibility is to serve the company by providing current critical, data and analysis of all activity affecting the financial parameters, in all parts of the company. This includes the forecasting of impending danger, vulnerability and weaknesses the company may face, be that purely financial or events and activities that might affect the future financial status of the company. The third responsibility is to encourage and promote fiscal responsibility throughout the company. This can only be done if the finance organization is fully integrated with the rest of the company. The forth responsibility is to forecast the companies finance needs, both ongoing and well out into the future. Anticipating needed financing can be critical to the profitable growth of the company.

More importantly, the finance organization should perform several roles with at least two operational purposes addressed. First, it needs to be the financial compass and custodian of all financial issues and practices. This includes setting the financial morality and legal limits under which the company operates. Secondly, it needs to extend its knowledge, disciplines and resources to serve and assist all areas of the company in any and all financial matters - even to those that believe they do not need it.

Another key financial organization responsibility is to continually forecast the cash flow to avoid shortages of operating money. It must anticipate shortfalls of receipts, unexpected emergency expenditures. New financial requirements and long-term needs must be addressed before they become critical. When your company is in a tight money situation, the cost of money goes up and in some cases it can become too expensive.

DO NOT UNDERSTAND THEIR MARKETS

A terrific product is a place to start, but it is only a beginning. Great products and services have languished in obscurity because of marketing ineptness, inexperience or the market was never really understood. In one sense, you have done little until you have created a demand for your product. *Marketing science is as important as any science that invents or builds the product*. Clearly then, it is imperative that experienced and talented marketing people are a high priority in any progressive company.

In most companies the product planner is usually the CEO or the founder. Because of this, it is no wonder that many companies go astray when the product planer leaves the company and moves on. It is unlikely that a start-up company would try learning marketing on the fly - but some do. That means that key marketing positions must be filled with people that are currently competent and ready to perform at an inspired level.

Knowing what the world will be buying three or five years form now is essential to developing and marketing successful products. The process of product planning is not guesswork, but it is not clear what makes a consistently successful product planner. Those people that possess this intuitive knowledge are, in my opinion, the company's jewels.

To illustrate the supper critical rolls that marketing and product planning plays in the success of an enterprise, consider this.

All dressed up and nowhere to go

Let us suppose that a company came to me and said, "Joe we are developing **Green Widgets** of the most advanced technology. We expect to introduce the product in eighteen months. We need you to build a company in Singapore to manufacture this product. It must be ready to go into high volume as soon as the product is released, but also in six months, you need to be fully organized and capable of producing reasonable quantities of subassemblies and parts for the "**Green Widget Product.**"

With my marching orders I proceeded to set up the company in Singapore. I hired one of the best management staff I have ever had. My engineering staff was highly experienced and technically capable as any in the U.S.A. In six months we were producing subassemblies and components of exceptional quality and they were cost effective as well. As the product release date grew near I increased the staff to meet the demands projected. The entire staff and work force was highly trained and ready for the challenge that lay ahead. We had met every schedule and target, and we were ready. Then one day I picked up the phone and the corporation CEO was on the line. He started talking:

"Joe, you and your team have done a fine job. We in corporate recognize the excellent organization you have put together. You and your staff are to be congratulated." Then he gave me the punch line. "We are sorry to have to tell you that our marketing strategy and product planning was wrong. The world is not buying *Green Widgets*; the world is buying *Red Widgets*. It is too late to change over to *Red Widgets*, so we missed the market altogether. Shut your operation down and on your way back, stop in for your severance pay."

There is one very strong message here that clearly needs to be understood. That is, no mater how well I built the company, no mater how well the staff and the troops were trained and no mater how good was the talent I hired, nothing maters if the world is not buying **Green Widgets**. It only matters that, first of all, the right product was envisioned, planned for and executed in the right time frame, and the world was actually buying it. Marketing and Product planning are the essential strategic tools that point the way. Granted, all the other business essentials must follow, **but the right product for the right time is everything.**

DO NOT UNDERSTAND THEIR EMPLOYEES

Bullheaded, indifferent, withdrawn, unreasonable or arrogant company management is the stuff that brings employee dissatisfaction, low moral, low productivity, high turnover, and sometimes the total brake down between management and the employees. Companies have failed because the management did not understand their employees.

There are always warning signs of belligerent or indifferent management practices. If these warnings are ignored, the fault belongs to the top management, the CEO, president and the chief executive. Managers and supervisors normally do not go off and practice a management style without some sign, direction or by example from the top. With few exceptions, employee unrest, dissatisfaction, or outright rebellion, is the fault of management.

DO NOT UNDERSTAND THEIR CUSTOMERS

A customer is a fragile, illusive, fickle, seldom faithful, often unreasonable and demanding business reality. Then, is it any wonder why customer turnover and dissatisfaction is seldom met head-on? We need to accept the fact that most customers are often difficult to deal with. In fact, some are next to impossible, but they are everything to your success. To better understand you customer we might gain some insight by look-ing in the mirror.

Your company is a supplier to your customers and, at the same time, a customer to those that serve your needs. How do you look to your suppliers? Are you ready to move to an-other supplier for a lower price, better service, more reliable product or because you have become frustrated? One way to better understand your customers is to examine the motivates of your own company and its own customer/vendor relation-ships. What do you expect from the suppliers who serve your company? Also, ask yourself: How faithful is your company to your vendors? Has, or would your company drop a long-standing vendor for a few percent lower cost? Or, if your long-standing supplier had an unexpected financial problem, would your company stick with him, maybe even try to help, or would your company quickly find another vendor? The point here is you might gain an insight into how your customers think by looking into the mirror. In many ways, you are not so different than your customers.

DO NOT HAVE ENOUGH MONEY

This is one of the most common reasons for failure. Start-ing out, many entrepreneurs grossly underestimate their need for money and that is often disastrous. The problem is that early planning is usually calculated on an optimistic level. The planners plan on a best-case scenario. When unseen problems develop there are no safety margins. When your funding is marginal, it is much more difficult to ride out the many un-planned things that go wrong.

Starting and building a company is a fairly courageous thing to do, it means taking risks at every turn. Being too tight with money will likely rein in some of that intrepid entrepreneurial spirit. Chances normally taken would likely be toned down or bypassed altogether. Most successful startup companies, looking back, feel that taking a chance was a normal, every day challenge. In fact, the startups I have been involved with were on a knife's edge most of the time.

The problem is made worse because banks, venture capitalists and other sources of money are more skeptical of a company in money trouble. Not only is the money difficult to come by but, any money obtained, under this cloud will likely be very expensive. If a choice was available, I would defer a startup if the initial financing was marginal, rather then risk failure and even more difficult money raising efforts the second time around.

DO NOT PROVIDE FOR KEY MANAGEMENT TRANSITION

Companies fail when key people leave and there is no suitable replacement. Very successful young companies often produce wealthy founders and key management people that cash in their stock options and move on soon after their first or second public offering. Key people like the CEO (who is often the product planner) and chief product architect, shape the course of the company. They have enormous influence and force behind the companies products, services and culture. When they leave it can be like a ship without a rudder or navigating with a defective compass. Investors should be well aware of the key people and what the potential is for losing them - for any reason. Management that operates in a mahogany vacuum may wake up one day to find the key people behind their company have evaporated and the investors, who they work for, are in for a rough ride.

DO NOT HIRE COMPETENT PEOPLE

Hiring the right people is one of the most important functions of the company. This is where decisions made affect the company far into the future. But, it may not seem like it is that serious of a task. After all, there is the resume, the references, your experience in hiring, and a detailed job description. That should insure the best selection out of the group that is competing for the job. However, it is more complicated then that.

My guess is that most managers have about a fifty percent chance on choosing the best person available. There are many reasons for this, but the most important reason is that an interview process is mostly a playacting game that is played on the interviewing stage. Both the interviewer and the interviewee are engaged in a game of matching wits and interview skills against each other. A good actor, a person really good at playacting can outsmart all but the best interviewer.

An interviewer with rigid values, preconceived ideas and convictions can end up hiring people that fit his or her guidelines but fail to provide the company with the most desirable people.

This brings up another problem. Your companies potential, capacity for growth and its durability are dependent upon the people that make up the company. In most companies the Personal or Human Relations Department have the greatest influence over who gets hired? Unless there is a check and balance, just a few people can influence the destiny of a company by designing the character and personality of the company.

Typically, the people with the final decision are the supervisors, managers or executives that the applicants will work for. However, in many companies the screening process decides who will get the interview. It is here we have a filter that screens out applicants that do not meet the criteria set by the Personal or Human Relations Department and more specifically that person in charge of interviewing and hiring. In companies where this influence is strong, the companies management mistakenly believes they are calling the shots.

In many companies the newly hired employee becomes a file in the personnel department after he or she is hired. Unless that person is discharged or promoted, there is little feedback to check up on the merits of the hiring process. One good way to learn how to hire a better staff is to have a *follow-up system* that tracks employees over the months and years to see if they turned out as envisioned when they were hired. Some personnel or human relations organizations would not eagerly endorse a system that could put them on the spot. But, there needs to be a way to identify a week hiring system. The company's soul and life force is at stake.

The problem is that there is no way you can know who was the best choice and who would have worked out best. What may happen is either the person chosen becomes a real performer or he failed to work out and had to be let go. Those are the two extremes. More likely the person chosen fits-in and becomes one of the acceptable employees. And that is, in itself, a successful employee acquisition – or is it? The only measure you have of being right or wrong is if a person turns out later to be a winner or a dud. But, what if most employees you were able to hire were a fit, That is they worked out OK. That would be a great employee hiring record. Just think of it, no misfits, no poor performers and no exceptional achievers: Just one happy family of acceptable employees. That would be a real accomplishment for the Human Resources and the principle hiring managers – or would it?. But, what kind of company would you have? It would likely be a less stressful place to work-unless it eventually failed because they drowned in the pool of its own mediocrity.

A DEEPER PROBLEM IS HIRING THE BEST AVAILABLE WHEN THE BEST AVAILABLE IS NOT GOOD ENOUGH

There are times, looking back, I would have considered hiring fifty percent good achievers is a reasonable track record. I know this sounds like a very low success percentage. But the truth is that many of the people we hire fall into the middle category of medeorcor employees. And, then there are times I began to believe I was a gifted manager because nearly everyone I hired seemed to be an above average achiever. The reason might have been the quality of the pool in which I was hiring. Hiring the best available is, in some ways, an achievement. However, if what is available is not good enough, a real disservice can be done. Recognizing this can be the force to break out of the box, even if it means bending some rules or accepted practices. I have on several occasions had a parade of aspiring candidates to interview and could not make a choice. I think at times I thought perhaps it was me. Was I asking too much? When this happened I had this little voice in the back of my mind that said" You need to throw a bigger loop, get out of this pool, break the rules if you have to but don't just choose someone, although they may be the best of this pool, ask myself, is this person really good enough?

HAVE LOST THE MISSION

Some companies start out with a firm grip on their mission and strategy only to lose it over a period of time. Management changeovers are the most common reason for the lost mission. Repeated management changeover will invariably rattle and confuse each successive management team to the point where the original mission can be lost completely and subsequent missions are unclear and lack force. Every new team needs to restate the company the company mission to complement their course of action and strategy, which often means lost momentum and often a new direction for the company.

Some time ago, I was asked to evaluate why this company had operations in South East Asia. The current management could not piece together a rationale for the offshore subsidiary they had inherited. They could not decide if the offshore operation. was a fit because that team had little experience with the business of offshore operations and what profit contribution they could expect. Several management turnovers had left few clues of the previous management strategy. The organizational structure was a jigsaw puzzle with no apparent logic to the structure.

What this new management team needed to do was to understand where they wanted to go and if the offshore operations was part of that picture. I asked them to state the mission that they envisioned. When the team did their homework it made my job easy. They basically answered the question themselves. It turned out that there was a good fit and the offshore operation was folded into their mission and strategy. Subsequently, the offshore operations made significant profit contributions.

DO NOT PLAN OR FOLLOW THEIR PLAN OR REVISE THEIR PLAN

Some entrepreneur's develop a business plan, and that is the extent of the planning effort. That plan is used to attract investment on the front end and then filed away until it is needed to attract more capital. A lot more could be derived from a good business plan with just a little more effort.

The business plan is just the beginning of the ongoing planning process. It is the model that the detailed planning or *Master Planning* is built on. Detailed planning, in some areas may need to be broken down into sub-plans and into even finer detailed plans. I have designed many startup Master Plans and in most cases, the detail consists of over three hundred action items. Each one contains a detailed portfolio and all are religiously tracked. This is essential to maintaining schedule and avoiding costly surprises. It is the details that can enable your success.

DO NOT DEVELOP, BALANCED BUSINESS FUNDA-MENTALS

In many companies, particularly young growing enterprises, there is often a disproportionate attention and fixation on the more glamorous elements of the business. Not all elements of the company are considered equal. In technical companies, the technology is usually the center of attention. In sales orientated companies, it is the Marketing Organization that the rest of the company orbits around, and so on. The problem is that other very important elements of the company may not get the attention that is necessary because they are on the fringe of company focus. The result can be ruinous.

For instance, in some companies the finance departments are just the people that pay the bills, check the expense reports and make payroll, but never seem to have the information the operations department needs. Yet, the finance organization is essential to the short and long term success of the company. If they are considered a second-class operation, top management may not look for the level of talent that would give the company the financial leadership it needs. Also, without appropriate prestige, their contribution would be downgraded and warnings of impending financial disaster would likely be dismissed or ignored. Finance is one of the fundamental elements of any enterprise. Other less glamorous parts of the company need to be a full partner also. The bottom line is that every part of the company is important. They all need to be appreciated and supported.

Another activity on the fringe of focus is the legal department. Legal issues are often left undone or patched together, hoping to be cleaned up later when more time can be devoted to the issues. Yet, a serious legal problem can bring a company to a standstill. Even small details can distract a company and cost them precious time and money. International legal issues need to be done right the first time. Cleaning up a legal mess in another country can be costly and time consuming and can hold up important programs and progress. Offshore legal issues are a special kind of problem because they often pop up as surprises and most companies do not realize how complex they can be.

It is clear that the reasons companies fail are not great mysteries that business science has yet to unravel. It is not complex science that will unlock the mysteries of enterprise success. We should know how to conduct business without making serious basic mistakes and omissions. And yet, far too many companies can't seem to get the most basic elements of business right. Without the basics of business under tight control, there is little chance for success and long-term survival.

Chapter III

THE VOICES OF FAILURE AND SUCCESS

Keep it Simple Stupid - because it is

I would suggest that the real reasons for success and failure are not well known or understood by some management experts. There are too many new definitions, labels, buzzwords, and wild theories that are used to explain failures and successes. The explanations and labels are getting more complex and academic. Labels are like wallpaper that often covers up the real, sometimes ugly, but usually simple, reasons for failure. Some people often miss the point when assigning blame for a company's failure because some of the reasons are as simple as these:

> The management was incompetent.
> The CEO's ego was responsible; he would not listen to anyone.
> They never really understood the business they were in.
> They never understood their customers
> They had a good idea but never figured how to make money.

They did not plan for enough finances.

The management was divided, divisive, political, quarrelsome and incompatible.

The board of directors barely touched on the ongoing vital business factors and was off kicking the hell out of mice, planning the company's transition into a mega-corporation.

When companies do fail, why do we hear an endless stream of complex, way-out reasons for failure? I will translate some of these lame excuses.

When failure strikes, we often hear excuses like:

"The market forces were out of step."

Translation: Our Product Planning was so bad, we missed the market all together.

"The competition had an unfair advantage, and they were lucky."

Translation: The competition had their act together – they ate our lunch.

"Bad timing."

Translation: Anytime would have been the wrong time to introduce that product. We did a poor job of analyzing the competition's products and market.

"We ran out of money."

Translation: No one was watching the bottom line and the cash flow projections. In addition, the sales forecast was a joke.

"The economy was a negative factor"

Translation: The economy didn't have anything to do with it but who is going to know now.

"The product was ahead of it's time."

>Translation: We had to bury this one; it was a bad product.

"No one could have prevented it. It was destined to happen."

>Translation: God gets the blame here, but they don't come right out and say it.

"The cost of doing business had gone sky-high. It was impossible to make a profit."

>Translation: We didn't manage manufacturing and material cost very well; we woke up one day and we were out of money.

"The government had it in for us, The IRS gave us a real bad time"

>Translation: Our accounting was so primitive we didn't even pay our taxes.

And so on and on, and more excuses you can count, but scarcely a word about the possibility that the management failed.

FROM A KERNEL OF TRUTH COMETH A SILO OF CORN

Some of these new management fixes and concepts have a kernel of truth, or originality, around which is the fabrication of supporting nonsense, often in academic filigree. Done well, it is attractive bait for desperate companies. However, some of these snakebite remedies can take the company further away from the real problems.

I remember early in my career, one such particularly academically appearing management discipline that took our company by storm. It was the rage of companies that wished their management to be viewed as innovative and forward thinking. Management did not participated in the studies. It appeared to us junior executives that the senior management thought they were above the need for it, however, it was required for us.

After a long period of study and lectures, it slowly became clear that the disciplines required would take years of practice to become natural and practical. One by one we dropped all pretense of using the discipline and went back to our own, individual modus operandi.

The damage from that experiment was unnecessary. We lost a measure of confidence in our management's judgment. Although this incident happened years ago, we are not without new and equally frivolous or impractical management concepts today.

A SUCCESSFUL FAILURE
(Not an oxymoron)

Is a successful failure like making gold out of lead?

Business failures are often like icebergs; you only see a small part of what is really there or what actually happened. Failures occur in many ways and a great deal of them are dressed up to look like successful mergers, consolidations, sell-offs of non-synergistic parts of the company, or buyouts and absorptions for various reasons.

A Successful Failure is one where the management has convinced nearly everyone, including lower level management, the shareholders and the customers that the failure is really a well-planned strategic maneuver.

FAILURE GOES MASQUERADING AS SUCCESS

It appears that the more colossal the foul up, the more believable the excuses. In fact, management seems to reach new levels of creativity and eloquence when it comes to sidestepping the responsibility and placing the blame on someone or something else. Read some of the press releases, quarterly and annual reports, and you could see some of the best window dressing and clever double talk that would make even Hollywood envious.

NOW YOU SEE IT - NOW YOU DON'T

A powerful tool is the finance organization. It can be used to disguise or transform just about any part of the company. Losers and winners are just numbers that can be manipulated. Corporate allocations can favor one product, department, operation or division over another. Charges for materials, services and products can be manipulated by transferring from one department to another. If a company was trying to sell a loosing operation it might start early by making favorable transfers to the operation they were trying to sell, leaving a profit where it makes the best impression and absorbing losses where they can not be seen. On the other hand, if someone decided to make an operation or its manager look bad, it would be easy. It can be done with a few strokes on the computer keyboard.

Having a short leash on the Vice President of Finance can be the CEO's passport to short-term success. The message here is: don't believe everything you hear or read. You should question the validity of management maneuvers and the purported brilliant strategy. They may be failures in disguise. A common misconception is that what you read in a P&L and

Balance Sheet is a fairly accurate portrait of the company's vital elements. It isn't necessarily so. Cooking the books is a practice on the rise. Cooking the books is where the numbers are bent, shaved, stretched, distorted, and manipulated to serve a purpose, either legal or illegal. Even when the numbers look reasonable, one must question the rules and methods used to assemble them. Sadly, the small number of convictions for illegal financial skullduggery and the lenient sentences reinforced the adage that crime does pay, and handsomely indeed.

In any case, intense scrutiny of accounting practices is essential because whatever the company does, well or poorly, the investors, the customers and the employees have a right to know what is really going on. That includes timely, accurate and truthful forecasting of impending danger. It is impossible to avoid eventual disaster unless the true financial status is known, understood and acted upon.

THE VOICE OF THE SUCCESSFUL

It is far more practical and productive to study failures than successes

I love to read about interviews with successful (at the moment) executives. Good grief, the babble that comes out of some of them. But, the interviewer and the world seem to hang on every word. In my opinion, interviewing most executives can be about as informative as talking to your bedpost.

> *Management testimonies are rarely valid for a variety of reasons. Find me an executive that was really in the thick of things and can be objective, and give credit and blame where it belongs, and I will show Diogenese an honest man.*

Never mind that the executive being interviewed and quoted has had three straight failures before this momentary success. Those were not his or her fault. Besides, a failure here and there is a sign that the executive has been through the mill and should be ready for the big game. If you are a manager or an executive and have had a recent failure or two, don't despair; you have at least seven lives left. With a few solid failures under your belt you are twice prepared for a better shot at it the next time. Besides, failure is, or should be, a learning process If it is, it is a very expensive education.

It's never easy to deal with failure and some people do it better then others. In any case, failure has to be addressed. On the other hand, adversity has a way of hardening our defenses and sharpening our perspective. Yet, with all the benefits of experiencing and surviving failure, there is usually a price that someone has to pay. Some people who fail go blissfully on, unmindful of the destruction left in their wake. Never mind the chaos, debris and carnage left behind, that is someone else's problem. Lost jobs, lost investments and the cost of starting over are only the beginning for those affected by a failed company. Their personal life is usually turned upside down.

THE MODEL FOR SUCCESS

What do really large– Mega size companies have to do with anything (except themselves and their competition) anyway? A great deal of research, and data gathering has been done on super companies, Fortune 500 size companies, about how they manage and how they achieved success.

Companies like IBM, Hewlett Packard, GE, ITT and Microsoft, are often the subject of intense scrutiny. There are many books written, quotations and executive interviews, all to reveal their secrets of success. The problem is, I don't believe there are more then a very few gifted people in the world who have the slightest clue how really large companies work, let-alone what made some of these companies superstars and why others failed. Most of these mammoth enterprises are running on their own momentum at an unchallengeable and uncontrollable speed that can neither be easily accelerated nor easily slowed down.

APPLES AND ORANGES

The priorities and focus of really large companies do not vaguely resemble that of a start-up, or of struggling small and medium size companies, which make up the largest part of the world's enterprises. Likely as not, the people who you talk to now were not around when the building blocks for success or failure were laid. The real question is: What do mega-companies have to do with the reality and the real world? Some of these companies have created a world of their own that they themselves do not fully understand.

Most obvious is that large – mega - corporations, and most other enterprises, are as different as the sun and the moon. As wise as man has become, he is yet to define how to make a General Motors, a Xerox, or a Bell Telephone. If we could, we would be inundated with these giants. Further proof of the mega-company mystique is that nearly every one of them has had near disaster experiences at one time or another, and many more have disappeared. How can that happen if we have valid blueprints for mega-corporations?

More to the point is that the chemistry, priorities and function of these giant companies are so different that they have almost nothing to offer a small and medium size company – lest it be sound management principles. It would be far more interesting to study a startup or a young middle-sized company as it battles more applicable and germane obstacles and challenges.

Yet, much of today's books and articles thrive on interviews of giant companies for clues about how these companies work. However, I believe what goes on inside some of these goliath originations is so mysterious, not even the IRS can pretend to know. Also, if there were pertinent and practical knowledge to be gained from these mega companies, it would be of practical value to only a handful of people in the world.

A POOR EXAMPLE

What really large companies often do is get away with policies and practices that would kill a small company. They get away with it because of their colossal momentum. They often make mistakes day in, year out and not feel the pain for years. They can carry excessive overhead and incompetent managers and executives indefinitely - and many often do. There are totally unrelated practices are often cited as important traits that contribute to the company's success. And, when observed from the outside, these policies and practices are often credited as reasons for their success. We are often overly impressed with a successful company's trivia, like when an executive wears blue jeans instead of pinstripes and a tie. The next thing you know, casual is in and formality is old stuff but that likely has nothing to do with the success of that company.

THE ALL-POWERFUL EGO

It may be difficult to accept, but enterprises are fragile entities. They can be brought down by something as common as a bloated executive ego. The contradiction is that many will argue that a sizeable ego is a centerpiece of a successful executive's repartee, and there is some truth to that. The problem is that an unchecked ego could be one of the main reasons behind enterprise failure; however, it is usually difficult to make that case. If it were possible to develop an ego index, it might be helpful in evaluating executives for hiring and promotions. But, there is still another problem; egos are a living part of the personality. I know this from first-hand experience. I watched a capable executive change into a completely self-serving, uncompromising despotic CEO In less then a year. I would never have guessed it could happen to him because I knew this manager from another company where he was an ideal executive on the way up. It is difficult to predict what success will do to people as they gain more and more responsibility, recognition, and power.

MOTORCYCLE RIDERS AND CEO'S

In at least in three important ways, CEO's and top executives are like motorcycle riders.

There are three kinds:

"The one's that are just getting up,
The one's that are just going down
And the ones that keep getting up
again and again and again"

LOSING THE MISSION

Another reason for failure is when a company loses the mission or never had the mission straight in the first place. An example of a company that had lost its way was a ten-year-old hi-tech Silicon Valley company. It had become a NASDEC favorite because it always made or exceeded it's profit projections.

The CFO was so conservative that he had amassed a bank of reserves that insured the profit each quarter matched his previous projections.

Over a three-year period the original management had slowly left, taking with them well deserved financial rewards from generous stock options that were now worth nearly ten times their original price. Naturally, their replacements did not enjoy similar stock appreciation potential and this began to affect policies and practices and profit strategy. First to change was their conservative growth strategy that achieved annual growth of 8% to 10% by controlled expansion. Now, under much more aggressive policies, the growth was driven by heavy borrowing and a rapid series of acquisitions.

Soon all the reserves had been used up to cover the now increasing losses due primarily to the inability to manage the new acquisitions. Presently, employees began to become suspicious when sales and shipments were dropping, but the numbers released to the public continued to show stellar performance. Unknown to the outside world, shipping records showed shipments that had never occurred. In some cases the shipments were real but they went to a secrete warehouse because the contents inside the boxes were bricks.

Stock price continued to rise and the paper value of the management's stock options improved beyond expectations. The problem here is management betting on a turn-around miracle. Then, the inevitable happened. Word leaked out that all was not well inside the company. Soon the banks stopped new loans. Customers became dissatisfied because of late deliveries and poor service. For the first time, Customer Service was difficult to reach by phone.

In a surprisingly short time the stock plummeted from $31 to $4.50 and the bottom was yet to come. A mere seven months later the company filed for chapter eleven. It was later theorized that the new management lost their way because of a serious lack of financial know-how. I believe the real reason was that no one at the helm knew where they were going. The founders failed to provide the transfer of both a business compass as well as a moral compass.

THE SUCCESS STYLE

It is easy to talk or write about problems and what is wrong about something, but it is much more difficult to say why it is, and what to do about it. Some business gurus write about the traits and practices of successful business people but I have trouble with some of that because we are complex people and what works for some may not work for others. Further, I have seen successful managers and executives break just about every rule in the book and come out smelling like a rose. That example is not recommended, but it is very tempting as evidenced by the increasing number of business scoundrels that are exposed every day.

As a result, I hold out little hope that there is a style, formula or discipline that we can latch on to that will propel us into greatness. Instead, I suggest that we go shopping, like we would for a new wardrobe. It would not do to buy cloths that don't fit or match you any more then you could adopt a management style that would work for you just because it appears to works for someone else.

Think back to your experiences where there was someone above you that you both admired and disliked. You may have admired his or her ability to solve problems but hated the way that person treated you and others. Or, you admired how hard your boss worked but you disliked being kept in the dark most of the time. It is hard to imagine liking every trait of someone so much that you would want to be his or her clone.

Having taken the position that you can't easily copy management styles, I do say there are axioms in business that can be the foundation for a flexible adaptation of styles that fit you, and that you can make-work.

The incredibly successful are a mystery to most of us, and I would believe that many of them secretly thank the heavens, fate, and luck for their success.

Far too many executives do not have a clue why they were successful, and others, why they failed

Chapter IV

SOME ESSENTIALS FOR ENTERPRISE SUCCESS

The elements of enterprise success are not found in catchy, fashionable slogans or seemingly profound statement of theory. We are sometimes impressed with management theory that is new and faddish. We also suspect that simple statements of fact are too commonplace to contain real truth and wisdom. And, too many managers and executives are searching for the silver bullet that will propel them on to the next management plateau - something that will tilt the management field in their favor. The sad reality is that there are few shortcuts, and those that promise quick success are either naive or insincere.

Today we are swamped with a whole new language and business lexicon filled with cyber space words and phrases and much of it is just nonsense. Some say that unless we understand this new lingo we are doomed to failure in this modern business world. We are also being told that there is a whole new way of doing business, even though some of these new concepts look strangely like the advice that great leaders have been giving us for years. Unfortunately, we need to understand it because much of it is code for the langue of the future.

SOMETHING TO THINK ABOUT

Here are some straightforward concepts and ideas that really work, and although nothing can insure success, these ideas can take you and your company a little closer to the winner's circle.

MANAGEMENT SOLIDARITY

More than just a few promising enterprises have been struck down from within, and the competition never fired a shot. Disharmony among managers and executives, stemming from greed, envy or politics, can bring a company to its knees as surely as running out of money. The affairs of the enterprise are severely impaired when management engages in subversive combat. It will eventually reach all levels of the company. Sides are taken and the preoccupation of employees, those involved and those not directly involved, take a toll in lost efficiency. The enterprise begins to slow.

The idea that a little competition between managers and executives is healthy is another old and outdated concept we can do without. When there is unrest and warfare at the top, the company stands still or pauses to watch it happen, and to contemplate the outcome. It would be unrealistic to expect employees to ignore the struggles when their future might be at stake.

The future of a company is never more in doubt than when the leadership is divided and has lost the common purpose. No matter how good the product or service, a divided management will cripple the company. Where politics and intrigue are allowed thrive, there will eventually develop a virus that will infect everyone involved, as well as some of the bystanders, and observers. Not only does it infect the company's vital organs, customers and vendors will also be drawn into the turmoil. Companies rarely succeed when the management is tearing each other apart. Someone has to step up to the bar and strike it down, and that is more effectively done by actions rather than words.

Abstaining from subversive politics is one way of showing maturity, character and leadership, however, sometimes is impossible to be neutral. Just being where you are determines if you are a member of the red or blue army. Like in the Shogun ways of old Japan, those on the losing side were all decapitated – if you have a choice, being on the winning side is much more fun.

The company management that knows that they can only succeed together has unlocked one of the doors to success. This is evident when there is solidarity of the management on important issues and decisions. In Japan, it is a cultural premise that the group comes first and apparent solidarity is the norm. In the USA it is more difficult to instill this kind of culture, but it is done in our own way, and it can be as strong as any in Japan. The President or CEO needs to make sure that members of his staff walk-the-walk because their actions are far more impressive and convincing then all the speeches and rhetoric ever used.

STAND TOGETHER OR FAIL

There are always different opinions and strong wills to be contested at the top of the management heap, but this interaction is best done in the executive catacombs where eventual consensus is a strong, clear message of management solidarity.

"No matter what transpires in the boardroom or in the executive staff meeting, when the company management comes out, they must be as one, united and mutually supportive. Do not think that the troops are unaware of a consensus or the lack of one. They will know, almost as it happens."

Managers and executives need to be seen as supportive and complementary of each other and there should never be a sly or veiled criticism of their fellow executives. To see your management as a solid force for the common purpose is like a shot of adrenaline; nothing short of success is as uplifting to the troops. In contrast, the management in trouble sends out signals of contradiction, discord and confusion, and when they bring their conflict out of the boardroom it reaches every part of the company.

Management body language is all too telling. People can detect the slightest sign of discord or disunity from management, and they are always looking for the signs. Once these signs are detected, people will begin to preoccupy themselves, take sides and involve others in speculating the worst. In the later stages the company can enter into the *Flocking Syndrome*; a topic I will discuss in another chapter.

Here is where a strong hand is needed at the top of the company. Assuming the chief executive is not the instigator, or part of the discord, he or she needs to step in and stop any conflict, even if it means firing most of the top management. It goes without saying that this sort of activity should not have gotten off the ground.

KILL THE VIRUS

Although there are many reasons for disharmony at the top, the reasons need to be brought out into the open at the appropriate level. Once a decision is reached, it must be acted upon, and any continued dissension stopped. Machiavelli made it clear that leaving behind unhappy and dissident factions will likely bring about eventual disaster. Make sure that everyone in the boat has picked up his or her oar and are eager to make the journey.

Many new CEO's and Presidents are often hired to replace those who could not cope with a management group at each other's throats. What works in this type of situation is not indecision, avoidance, timidity, patronizing, or permissive management. What works is careful, but urgent analysis, backed up by swift and certain action.

LEADERSHIP BY EXAMPLE

Nothing inspires like a leader or manager that really leads – out front and showing how to do it every day. That takes a great deal of mental and physical energy. All companies need management with tireless drive and focus of purpose, but especially those that are growing fast. In my opinion, the physical age of the leaders is not necessarily a barrier. You can see that in companies where the seventy-year-old leader consistently wears out his staff, some of whom are half his age. The essential ingredients of great management leaders are: drive, confidence, people skills, experience, applied intelligence, and honesty.

Every day the leader needs to project a high level of energy and pace. His followers will for the most part take up the challenge. A company can easily achieve three times the progress if they know what is expected of them - even if it is unreasonable.

THE FIRST TO SACRIFICE

If you expect your employees to make sacrifices, the management should show the way. If cuts in salaries are required to lower cost, the CEO and executives should be first to receive a smaller paycheck. More than that, the cuts should be deeper by percentage than the employees so that the act cannot be seen as a hollow gesture. Dealing out stock options and raises when the company is struggling and people are sacrificing, is idiotic, but it happens when executive management is out of touch with the real world.

There are always times when extra effort must be made to meet a deadline, support a customer, make an important production schedule, or introduce a new product on schedule. Certain parts of the organization are going to be called upon to put forth extra effort, like overtime, extra travel, or longer hours. Working around the clock is not unusual for upper management. To go the extra mile for the company the management should consider it a privilege to unhesitatingly go the extra mile, put in the extra effort and that should be the norm, not the exception.

BODY LANGUAGE

In my younger days in lower management I learned a lesson that is worth passing on. As a manager or executive you have the responsibility to project a positive attitude by all means, including body language. Few managers understand how closely their subordinates are watching them. If you come out of your office with a scorn or worried look on your face, you are passing on a great deal of anxiety to the troops. Just your expression is enough to start people whispering, and the next thing you know the people are flocking at coffee breaks in the bathrooms and in the halls. Your worried expression may have been because your dog is sick or your car is acting up or you woke up with a stiff neck, but they don't know that. On the other hand you may have just come out of a meeting of company executives, and it was brutal in there. That look on you face, the bent posture and preoccupied stare are all too telling, - they will know. What I learned was to keep my feelings to myself and get on with the job of fixing the problems.

When I stepped out of my office, to a meeting or on to the manufacturing floor, I knew my every action my body language carried a message - and I learned to send the right message – most of the time.

The bonus for projecting a positive bearing is that it also works on you, yourself. It seems odd but it can't help but affect you. It may have started out to affect the employees but it will affect you also.

TENACIOUS STATUS MANAGEMENT

Tracking and Review Resulting in Mission Redesign and Adjustment

Here is another point that I believe in completely. The process of tenacious tracking and constant readjustment of all the business elements is essential in the fast moving business world. Project management is not unlike a company management process. It is the tenacious tracking and adjusting of hundreds of issues and tasks that must happen minute-by-minute, hour-by-hour, every day. A sloppily managed project is a sign of a sloppily managed company.

When a new project is planned or an ongoing project is assessed, there are countless unexpected problems that pop up. Schedules are missed, costs go out of control, and confusion is rampant Unless you have that project in complete focus and in great detail, the project will likely encounter numerous delays and unforeseen obstacles. It is not uncommon to design a project control system with over five hundred line items that are reviewed every day, mostly by exception. Part of successful project management is designing the outcome. Not everything is predictable but if ninety percent or more of the elements are tracking and under control, you will have time to solve the few percent that are out of line.

MANY PROJECTS FAIL BECAUSE THE PEOPLE INVOLVED DO NOT UNDERSTAND THE DETAILS.

THE MISSION STATEMENT

We hear a lot of jokes and negative comments about *Mission Statements* and Strategy and how companies can do without them. In general I agree, but that is just too simple. We *do* need to project a message about where we are going and to some degree, how we are going to get there - at least in the short term. Success is not defined by just the end result. You have to find your way there. That takes more than just a fancy statement of the end objective, which is what many mission statements are. Yet, without some clear idea about your mission, it is likely the company could drift from the intended objectives.

Still, it is not necessary to have it engraved in bronze and hung at the entrance of *Mahogany Row* to remind the executive staff or to impress visiting customers. Or is it really effective to have it plastered all over the company on bulletin boards and posters in the hallways and bathrooms? The best way is to have the president or CEO, the executive level and management express the goals and progress directly to the company employees - frequently. This needs to be done often so that the status and future course of the company is clear to all and minor changes and deviations are understood. There are several problems with stated and displayed mission statements. If they are too broad and lofty like:

> **"We will strive to be the best company for our customers and our employees through excellence of quality products and dedication to serving our customers..."**

This is not quite as bad as a specific mission such that it soon becomes obsolete because of the companies change in direction or because of variations in growth. My preference is not to have a document type of mission statement but the management expresses the mission every day, in many ways.

Not everyone in management and at the worker level can or should translate a Mission Statement into work situations or decisions in the work place. Sometimes some of us get the opportunity to do that but that is not why Mission Statements are needed.

WHERE DID WE LOSE IT?

Some companies have lost the vision or mission altogether. This often happens because of management turnover; the vision or mission the new management has no respect for the outgoing management. After all, the new management is replacing the old management; therefore what they were doing before must not have been that good.

The new management is usually cocky and spends little time trying to understand what has happened and where the company was going - right or wrong. After successive change-overs with incomplete missions or missions cut short, no one knows what the mission is anymore. Finally someone has the presence of mind to ask:

"What the hell are we doing?"

One such company comes to mind. On this occasion I was hired by a company to find out what they were doing with operations in a particular Southeast Asian country. The present management had inherited a company that had developed into a broad marketing and manufacturing, a multinational company.

They knew what they had, but had no idea why or how it got to be what it was. They were afraid to tamper with it even though they were losing money in some of the operations. They were afraid if they did the wrong thing, everything could come down on them.

I was asked to assess the merits of their Southeast Asian operations, which I did, but not before I asked the executive staff to do some homework of their own. I asked them to define their present business plan and relate that to the offshore operation. If it did fit, fine, but let's not have the tail wagging the dog. It turned out that they did need the offshore operations. What they did, in effect, was to rediscover a portion of the previous management's vision and mission. They didn't justwhack it because they did not understand it, they redefined their mission independently, and the offshore operations fell into place neatly.

MANAGEMENT CONTROL DEVICES

What if you could run your company and all its functions from your computer? That is just what the thousands of computer programs are trying to tell you. You can buy programs to predict, analyze, compare, examine, scrutinize, peruse, scan, explore, review, investigate, probe, audit and then there are programs that even check other programs. The problem is it's not that easy to know what you are getting into when you introduce a program into your company.

Unless someone in your company is very swift about computer systems and has very broad business knowledge, you have a poor chance of choosing the right programs for your company. The salesman will sell you the Brooklyn Bridge if he can. And, the more programs that become available, the worse it gets. There are some rules I follow that can help. First, I do not let an Information Manager or Systems Data Manager, or anyone not from the operation to be used for, make that decision alone. It is not unusual for a department or division to wake up one day to find that *someone up there* has decided on a control system you need that is often is too complex, too broad, too narrow (rarely the case), doesn't fit and will take money and time we don't have to implement it. By the way, *the someone up there* I am referring to is seldom top management because they often dodge the responsibility and avoid getting involved in the information systems decisions, until it doesn't work, even though the company could succeed or fail depending on some of these decisions.

Demonstrable managements elements like: Check lists, Gantt charts, tracking systems, marketing management spread sheets of endless types, analysis systems for every activity in the company and schedules are available to do your work for you. Actually, that is the problem Most of these devices do not do the work for you. The problem is that your company employees have to learn these new systems and that means change.

We already know that change is difficult to implement, control and maintain. Some of these new systems take years to become fully implemented, bug free, and adapted to the best way the company needs to function. The danger is that the company is forced to operate the way the systems were designed to work. That can be dangerous because it forces to change from what they know to something they are trying to learn. What often happens is a mixture of the new and old systems. Something never intended.

The most common failing of these tools is they are often left to fall behind and become out of date. Once the newness has faded, the disciplines necessary to keep them up, and reflecting reality become shoddy, they no longer serve the company. Once this happens the general attitude is to ignore them or worse yet hold them up to ridicule. Management loses face and the confidence in people at all levels. Employees become cynical. Once this happens it is difficult to rally the troops again with enthusiasm.

ALL THAT GLITTERS IS NOT GOLD

This may sound strange coming from one who has made his livelihood in the high-tech world, but bear with me for this thought. The computer systems and software available today are so powerful and compelling that we often fail to understand the danger they can inflict. Business software has become so powerful it can perform hundreds and even millions of operations and functions in the blink of an eye. Most of these are transparent and seamless. This means we do not see how many of the results have been derived and we are often in the dark about the premises and rules that produce these results. On the surface it sounds great because we are not burdened with all the details behind the data and information the computer provides.

Far too often the computer is responsible for a disaster like sending out a purchase order for two million parts that should have requested two hundred parts. Or purchase orders were issued to support production of fifty systems per month but should have ordered enough parts for five thousand systems per month. This resulted in canceled orders and severe loss of revenue and customer confidence. There are built in safeguards but they too are often not fully understood and implemented.

INFORMATION MADNESS OR INFORMATION POLLUTION

Not everyone needs to know everything about the mission or the state of the business or long-range strategy, or the competition's grip on the market. In fact, it is often better that some levels of company employees do not know much more than what their job requires. These may be people who are struggling to keep up with their job or are trying to learn their job. Bombarding them with tons of information can be distracting and does little to support the employees who do not need the distraction.

This statement flies in the face of the people who preach to employees with an inundation of information because it is supposed to make them a better employee. Balderdash! That is another way of *kicking the hell out of mice.* What often happens is that management does not know the difference between essential information and *static*. The message is that management needs to deliver essential information in large doses and in creative ways, but discriminate the static. Information on many subjects should be available to everyone in the company who wants it and needs it. When an employee requests specific information, the company should make it available unless it is sensitive. But I do not believe that it should be forced-fed to all employees. Essential information that is critical to the welfare, productivity and safety of the employees is imperative. But, for the average person, there are limits to the amount of information that can be processed and used efficiently. It is also true that too much information turns into static and that is distracting.

I don't believe that static is helpful to anyone except the people that are putting it out. For the most part, these people truly believe they are doing the employees a service. It is not uncommon for information to be selected and disseminated by lower level managers and supervisors who may not comprehend the significance of their choices of the information. Then, too, it is important not to slide from information to propaganda. Again powerful forces are afoot in the dissemination of information. It needs to be defined and monitored by upper management, Coming up the ranks I remember when I was an electronic technician going to college at night, or working nights and attending classes in the day, raising a family and making a living. I was exposed to what I needed to learn and do a good job and not much more. I excelled in time and moved up the ladder, and each time I was promoted my scope and areas of knowledge increased and widened, not excessively but as I was ready to take it in. Looking back, I am grateful that my management had the wisdom to know what I needed and when. They did not drown me in massive detail about things I had no control over or things that did not help me pursue my mission and learning process. As the result, the company received my best efforts and I grew and prospered in a planned and controlled manner. That was a classical win-win situation.

YOU MUST BE PART OF THE CULTURE

We call it being part of the team but it is really more than that. It is giving up just a little part of your individuality for a membership in a group-force with a common set of objectives. You may have to set aside some of your individuality if it is in conflict with your present business culture. It is also possible to favorably influence the team with your personal contribution, but only if you are accepted by the group.

You are a part of the group, or you are a stand alone individual and you will fail if you insist on standing outside the group. Whatever the reason, be it because you don't fit in with what is going on, or your ego needs or demands separation from the group, you can't contribute to the group. You need to get in or get out, there is no in-between.

Enthusiasm and eager support are your dues to the group, and you pay it every day. This holds true if you are a part of the middle management, in the executive ranks or part of a workman's group.

YOU CAN HAVE IT BOTH WAYS

The dilemma is, "how can I succeed unless I stand out from the crowd?" You can have it both ways. You can stand out by standing in. Being good at what you do and being supportive of the group makes you an overall standout along with the group. If you are not looking for accolades and praise you are likely going to have both.

Some people kid themselves and others by using disagreements as a mask for their deep-seated need to be contrasted, and much of this is because of insecurity. This is a losing situation for the individual and the group, and sometimes for the company. The Japanese culture is much more group indoctrinated and this is a distinct advantage in this context. Americans are often looked upon as commandos, and cowboys or loose cannons by some foreign business cultures. Although often true, is doesn't have to be that way.

PERSONAL CONSTRUCTIVE ATTITUDE

All the education, advice and business knowledge in the world will not help you if your head is not screwed on right. Attitude, in a close social system like a company, is as obvious as the clothes you wear. It is out there for everyone to see. It is the most important attribute you possess, but only if it is used in a positive way. A positive attitude is not just nice to have; it separates the habitual complainer, the non – performer, the cynic and the eternal skeptic from the can-do people who are most followed and admired.

I know it made a pivotal difference in my life. Early in my industrial career I came into a situation that was not healthy. The department was polarized and hostile to performers and newcomers like myself. Early on I had a run-in with the self appointed leader of the department. I had exceeded the normal output for my operations. I was told to slow down or the group would make sure I would be sorry. I soon found out that being sorry meant; I was to be isolated in every way. There was no one to have lunch with, no conversation with my fellow workers, and most disturbing were the false rumors about my family and me. It hurt, and I became bitter because it was so unfair. My work began to suffer and I took my frustration home with me. Now, I had all my waking hours consumed by this bitterness and the people responsible were in control.

Then one day at work, I suddenly realized what the problem really was. It was not these people who were responsible for my misery - it was me. My attitude was all wrong, and I was making my own hell.

From that point on I started talking sense to myself - and I listened. What I had to do was lift myself above the petty department politics and think on a mature and logical personal level, and on a broader company plane. In a matter of weeks, the tide turned. At first it was just the little things but later on I was confided in and sought out for advice by the very people that had previously tormented me. Soon thereafter, I was promoted.

Here is another example of attitude control. This company was an old-line company that had done well in low-tech products but had shifted gears and was introducing new high tech products for the first time. A long time supervisor had recently died and left a large gap in the marketing product sales. Someone was going to be promoted.

There were two candidates that were qualified, one more than the other. The most qualified man had a good track record, higher education and reached his position almost effortlessly. He was confident and likable but distant to those not his peers. The other candidate was younger and she had reached her position with tireless effort determination and a strong personal magnetism. People were drawn to her and she led them with a light hand and by her example of determination and performance. She won the promotion and the consensus was that her radiant personality infected everyone she came in contact with, which obliviously included her superiors. Education and track record are not everything. People have to believe in you.

IMPATIENCE IS NOT ALWAYS A BAD THING

Impatience is not so bad if you are basically impatient with yourself. Being impatient with the job, the environment and your boss is rarely productive. Being impatient with yourself can be productive. A certain amount of dissatisfaction and anxiety can provide the push, or pull, to move yourself off that plateau on which you are stuck. My advice is, don't blame anyone but yourself for where you are in life. You are the one in charge, if you are not, take charge.

Chapter V

TEAMS - A POOR SUBSTITUTE FOR MAKING IT HAPPEN

The word team is used today to define just about any group of people, of any size, working together. They could be a football, baseball, or a basketball team. Teams are not confined to sports. We have news teams, teams in business, teams and in the miltary of every imaginable type and teams in every human endeavor. What this chapter is about is a special use of the word team we use in business. The term team I am referring to might be more correctly called a **Special Team** created to resolve a special problem or unusual situation, or a generic issue that does not seem to fit in any particular department or segment of a company. Special Teams are usually formed out of frustration when upper management has tried the normal resources and they have failed to resolve the issue.

Special Teams, by their very nature, are less efficient than, let's say, a project group. That statement will make waves in some conventional minds, but it is easily defended. Consider one manager or executive that knows the answers to the problems or issues and knows the course of action required. He or she can quickly organize a project group and point the way.

It is often presumed that these teams will, with their collective brainpower and collective experiences, more efficiently serve the mission. The problem is that most special teams possess *collective redundancy* because most people have similar education and work experiences. Just one person that has the special knowledge, skill or capability can outperform many people who do not have it. Forming a special team in hopes that numerical magic will solve the problem is, in my opinion, a mistake. The all-important requirement is to have the services of people who have the knowledge and experience to lead the way. There is really no adequate substitute for experienced and talented people.

Special Teams often turn into committees that replace action with endless meetings and foot dragging, haggling and disharmony. The other problem is the lack of individual accountability. There is not that demanding ownership and accountability that individuals should have. In a team, the responsibility is spread over several team members rather then where to blame should be.

A SERIOUS STEP

The decision to organize a special team is a serious step, because now, in addition the problems you want the team to address, you have the dynamics of a complex social group to organize, direct, motivate and watch closely (A culture within a culture – so to speak). Not surprisingly, there can be meeting after meeting with the dynamics of a committee that often breaks down into bickering, positioning, and foot dragging.

Some of these teams fall apart because they lack direction or have poor leadership. Lack of direction can happen because the team usually has been empowered by upper management, and told to go off and solve the problem. The Management often sits back waiting for things to happen, in the belief that they have done their part. This type of management detachment is often the reason why teams flounder or fail. The other risks are predicable. Unless the team shows progress and improvement early on, there will be disappointment and dissolution. Now, you can have a de-motivated group that is experiencing failure, and the original problems are still there or have grown worse.

THE EMPOWERED TEAM

There are ways to energize, inspire and impart greater degrees of freedom without empowering a team. There is significant risk that a loosely supervised or unsupervised team will make and execute flawed decisions. When this happens management has few options, none of which are good. They can overrule the team, disband the team, discipline the team, etc, etc. In any case the outcome will not be pleasant.

The risk of letting a team make independent decisions is too high to be contemplated, except perhaps in very special situations. I also question: Why would management do that? Is it an effort to peruse social correctness in the workplace by democratizing the work process? Could it be that it is an attempt to galvanize the employees into a more efficient workforce by giving them the authority to make independent decisions? If so, it is a clumsy effort at best.

In my opinion setting up teams is not the way to energize and inspire your work force. I try to hire or assign people to groups who are already inspired, and are eager to tackle the project. If there are those that are waiting to be inspired, or empowered, I f likely have the wrong people involved.

NOT EVERY MANAGER CAN MANAGE A TEAM

Skilled team leadership is essential if the special team is to be successful. However, team leaders are not easy to identify unless they have a track record. Team leadership is a special management lore not every manager or executive has. If a team is poorly managed the repercussions are likely to be very serious.

Selecting a team leader can be difficult. Aggressive and decisive managers may not be the right people to manage a team. It takes a lot of patience and the ability to work with all kinds of people. In addition a team a manager should have several and flexible manager skills. He needs to be a coach who can encourage and motivate team members when the going gets tough. He also needs to have the experience to see the path ahead long before the team members have a clue. That can mean he needs to gently, but firmly, guide the team at or before critical times. These and other skills are not necessarily what made these high-performers successful. Team leadership is not as commonly practiced, as is the autocratic management style. Many good and effective managers I know would not be the best choice to lead a team.

It is not to say that teams can't be useful, they can and have done some remarkable things. I was on a team that did just that. We turned a major operation around that had been considered a lost cause. The experience was electric. The problem is that, I think my experience was an exception. Looking back, I have tried to identify why that team was so successful and why others failed. I think these were the key reasons for the success of that team:

> We had limited autonomy
> The team was given very limited autonomy in the beginning and as we matured we were given more. The original objective stayed in focus. The team had to earn autonomy; it was not just given because we might have wanted it.
>
> It was clear from the beginning that there was separation of church and state in that the mission was defined by the management, and the team's job was to figure out how to make it happen. We did not have the option of tampering with the company's strategy, nor did we want it.
>
> There were decision reviews of our work, which meant the team leader monitored most of our work and decisions, although not in an intrusive way. If he found something that didn't look right, he would share his concern with us and ask us to go look at it again.
>
> He gave us space when we asked for it, like sometimes we did not want him to be present at some meeting because we wanted to work out the issues ourselves. We learned and grew in competence because the team leader took the time to explain why some of our decisions were good, and in some cases, not the best we could come up with.
>
> Looking back, our leader was something special. He had that inner confidence that allowed him to lead without appearing to do so.

A backward looking critique convinces me that we were successful because of his rare blend of Autocratic, consolatory, participative, and instructive management style. That team leader kept us from shooting ourselves in the foot several times. He gave us the reign when we were capable of using the authority wisely.

Over the years I have seen teams that failed to complete their mission or fell short of the mission's original goals. An example was:

It was in Silicon Valley at a medium size company who, after a reasonable successful eleven years, had six loosing quarters in a row. Management had tried several approaches to stemming the red ink but nothing made a noticeable improvement. The problem was a broad slowing down of sales, rising manufacturing costs and customer dissatisfaction because of late deliveries and poor quality. The CEO decided enough was enough, so he directed the executive level to organize several teams, one each for marketing, manufacturing and Quality control. Each VP selected his team from the operations they would work on, in other words team members from Manufacturing were chose to work on problems in manufacturing the exception was the Marketing team.

Team leaders were chosen out of the manager's pool. A few were looking at having their teams assigned to solve problems that they themselves had previously been involved with-possibly responsible for. As the teams began to become organized, they grappled with selecting areas of interest to attack. This was difficult because some teams could not agree on what problem areas were the most important. An example was the Manufacturing Team who finally agreed on Production Control as their area of opportunity.

This team theorized that late delivers were caused by parts shortages, difficulty in organizing special orders and the capacity of some equipment that was often over scheduled. Having finally agreed on the areas to be attacked, they set off to fix the problems.

Because of the diversity of the team members there was little agreement as to how to fix them. After several weeks of debate they agreed that the core problem was the old production control computer program that was not very flexible, and an equally out of date purchasing computer program that ordered the parts.

The team then called in the department Managers of Production Control, and presented him with their findings.

The expected happened. The Manager of Production Control responded by strongly disagreeing with the report findings. Although the team's findings were expressed in a polite and inoffensive manor the PC manager would have none of it because it did, after all, point the finger at his operations. This resulted in a total deadlock. Management was called in to resolve the deadlock. After some time, the management persuaded the team to drop the recommendation. This had a divesting effect on the teams moral. Not long after that the team was dissolved. This is a case where the management did not have the guts to accept an obvious shortcoming because it might cause problems.

The Marketing team did not fare much better. The team mission was to find out ways to improve customer satisfaction and boost sales. Warranty and field service issues were focused on. The source of the information came from customer complaints and recorded complaint phone calls.

There was no marketing person assigned to the marketing team. This was a mistake because the credibility of the investigation was in question from the beginning. The unfamiliarity with marking terms and customers made the findings amateurish at best. When presented to management, it was clear that the report findings could not be implemented; they had no credibility.

The team chosen for quality control was to investigate way to improve customer satisfaction. The first approach was to tightening the inspection sampling to catch more defects. In one month there appeared to be a slight improvement in the products reaching the customers, but it was not enough. Then the team hit upon the idea to go out to the customer and see first hand the quality of the product from the customer's point of view. The effect was eye opening. For the first time they saw what the customer saw and first hand understood the reaction of the customer.

The team then made another productive deduction. They began to understand that catching defective products was after the fact. What they needed to do was stop the defects where they happened. This resulted in a complete change in the structure of the Quality Control Department and a dramatic improvement in the quality of the products reaching the customers.

Hear is an example of three teams that tried to act outside of the company management structure. One was somewhat successful. The other two efforts were actually negative in the overall efforts of the enterprise. The Thirty three percent success score sounds about right.

Now that I have fully enraged many who are happy and successful team members and team advocates, let me point out that there are many situations where teams are not only right, but they can be essential. In defense of teams, they can bridge groups, departments or divisions. They can bring much needed information and perspective to a problem. Teams can assemble a wide range of people with the required specialized knowledge. Where cross knowledge is limited or outdated, team members from other groups may possess valuable information that is essential for solving the problems and introducing policies and procedures that cross lines. There are other opportunities for teams such as training a team group that will disperse when the team has completed their tasks and the group will be interfacing from different departments or divisions. The team comradeship and close working relationships could be invaluable for ongoing operations. Team applications that require close coordination are obvious and many.

It would not be out of the question to form a team for the sole purpose of improving working relationships. Getting groups, departments, and individuals to unanimity and single purpose commitment. However, the same risks I previously discussed are also present here. The team must not be allowed to sink into a do-nothing committee with endless meeting and general dissent. Once the company has committed to a team solution, management must give it all the support it needs to be successful. It cannot be allowed to fail. Support also means constructive oversight.

TEAMS - CULTURES WITHIN A CULTURE

A company's culture is a difficult thing to establish and control. Some company cultures just evolve and sometimes to the detriment of the enterprise. So, when you deliberately create another culture inside the company culture, you are inviting more complications. *A team is a culture within the company culture.* It had better be a positive and productive culture.

However, sometimes a team can become a disruptive element. This can happen when the team develops a self-serving agenda or seeks to perpetuate or advance itself.

The problem is usually the lack of oversight. Once a team has been authorized and is operating, management often backs off, having created this extraordinary management entity, it presses on with the other business of the corporation.

PROJECT MANAGEMENT VERSES THE TEAM

Project management is a very efficient management tool because it is usually comes complete with time tested structure, style and form. The minute a project is formed it can be off and running. The project structure is pre-known, organizing is quickly accomplished and execution can swiftly follow. Contrast that with a team being formed, organizing itself, defining the rules, laying out the tasks and objectives, becoming failure with other team members and basically getting organized. Sure, some of these start up functions need to happen with a project as well, but much of it is pre-known by the project leader and therefore can happen in much less time.

The problem is that Project Management depends on an experienced manager or executive to plan, organize and execute the task, and he or she should not try to share that task with any other task or responsibility. Project management responsibility is serious business regardless of its scope and size. It is, almost without exception, a full time job.

How do you choose a Project Leader, and who does the choosing? Also, do you choose someone from inside the company or do you go outside? These are difficult questions and specific issues that cannot be dealt with here except in general terms. Generally, the person who the project leader will report to should choose him or her. Further, the person chosen needs to be a heavy weight with people skills and a track record. Most of all, the chosen one should be given an opportunity to outline the strategy and basic plan he or she intends to follow. Here is an opportunity to look inside that persons mind and reveal just who this person is and what is the style and strategy he or she is likely to employ. I also look for independent thinking ability because he or she will be moving fast and there is usually little time for lengthily and frequent consultation.

> *Getting people to work together does not mean you have to form a team to achieve teamwork, and in my opinion, if you can foster teamwork without a team, you are far better off.*

Chapter VI

Delegation - the Miracle Worker?

Somehow, the empowerment and delegation revolution has raised expectations to they point where we have come to expect near miracles from otherwise normal, average people. Delegation and empowerment do not make people smarter, wiser, more efficient, or more intuitive.

DELEGATION, EMPOWERMENT, MOTIVATION AND ALL THAT JAZZ

Just about every other management book you find will say something about delegation. Many will tell you that you need to do it - lots of it. It is written somewhere in the ten commandments of enlightened management that managers must delegate if they hope to be successful. There is so much wrong with this. Yes, I know this fly's in the face of most management experts, but this is a process that has the potential to do considerable damage unless skillfully employed.

Delegation may be the most misused, and misunderstood, management tool in the management business. As a trouble-maker, it is right up there. This delegation belief belongs to the long list of right sounding, but misleading management motherhood, management axioms, and buzzwords handed down from one generation to the next.

HOW ARE YOU GOING TO CLIMB THE CORPORATE LADDER IF YOU DON'T DELEGATE?

The most common and dangerous perception that many managers believe is that they are expected to delegate if they are to be perceived as executive material, and in many companies this is true. Executives practice irresponsible delegation because they either do not know any better, they think they are doing the delegate and or the company a service or they see it as an image building practice. In any case, it is expected that promising managers and executives delegate. However, that may be precisely the wrong medicine for companies at critical times. It is also ill advised to delegate to people who are not yet ready. That statement seems logical, but the problem is knowing when someone is ready. Sometimes all you can do is an extensive review of the candidate's background topped off with a good gut call. Even then you don't really know until you see the person in action. A fragile company is vulnerable to the experimentation and learning process that often comes with delegation. This is especially so with start-ups and struggling companies that can ill-afford mistakes.

TO DELEGATE OR NOT TO DELEGATE THAT IS THE QUESTION

What is wrong with delegation? Nothing, if done very carefully, with the right people, in the right environment and if the timing is right, and if the person doing the delegation understands his or her responsibility, and, if they have the time to keep close tabs on how the delegate is progressing. But, even if we are very careful, it is not guaranteed that the delegation will be successful. Perhaps not, so let's look at the act of delegation.

Delegation is a very complex process. The definition of the word delegation should give us a clue that there is much going on here. A denotation is: *"The act of empowering to act for another."* The empowering part is where it gets interesting. Another denotation of empowering is "to authorize" or "to give authority."

Part of what makes this difficult is that very few managers or executives are likely to give authority to anyone unless they are forced to. So what really happens is the giving of authority is usually on a limited basis, or with conditions attached. The result can often be a confused delegate, an indecisive delegate that is more likely to fail.

There are many reasons for delegating, some of which are admirable and some not so as we can see in what follows:

FOLLOWING TRADITION
PASSING THE BUCK
SETTING SOMEONE UP FOR FAILURE
ABDICATING RESPONSIBILITY
ACTING LIKE AN EXECUTIVE
GETTING THE JOB DONE

Delegation can be the transfer of responsibility, sometimes with authority, but more often without or with limited authority. It can be a transfer of a mission to accomplish a specific task or act, and it can be specifically directed or given cart blanch as to how it is to be carried out. It can be outlined, or assigned in specific detail. Progress can be required to be reported in great detail or left to carry on independently. It can be without penalty or with serious consequences if the mission fails. In other words, delegation comes in many different forms and for that reason there is considerable opportunity for the process to go wrong.

Delegation runs the gambit from:

> *"Do this exactly the way I tell you and I will tell you what you need to know."*
>
> *to*
>
> *"I don't care what you do or how you do it - just make it happen.*

SHOT IN THE FOOT

Consider the complexities for both the ones doing the delegating and the delegates. There are no rules and even if there were, too few managers would take the time to follow them – even if there was a right way. But, the problem is that not all managers and executives are knowledgeable enough or sufficiently skilled to insure successful delegation, one that fulfills the mission and keeps the delegate from shooting himself or herself in the foot.

There are some interesting types of delegation; one is *"The Autocratic Delegation."* This example occurred in Hong Kong but it can happen anywhere:

> The company is a typical young electronics company making a range of Telecommunications and computer products. They design products in Hong Kong and do most of the manufacturing just over the boarder in China.

The president is the founder and has experience working in British, local Chinese and American companies. In recent years, the young company was growing at better than 14% per year, compounded. This company is performing at better than 18% profit – after taxes. Sales are a little over fifty million US$. Consider this:

The president comes to work to be greeted by his staff who are Vice Presidents – all nine of them. They report the progress of their delegated tasks, careful to report yesterday's happenings in the context of their instructions. At the end of each narration, the president gives new instructions for that day, and receiving his instructions, each Vice President leaves immediately showing his enthusiasm to get on with his mission. Each day the scenario is repeated, except when one of the vice presidents fails to follow instructions or to get the right results. The president effectively skins the VP alive - in front of his colleagues. The smallest deviation from their instructions is an invitation to disaster.

In just eleven years the company became a world known front-runner and highly profitable company that is still being managed exactly the same way. The vice presidents still report everyday, in the same way, except there are only five original VP's. Two were fired for excessive illnesses – ulcers I'm told.

There are several points to be made by this example. First, the *Delegation* practiced here is not the storybook style most managers and executives would condone. Some would call this a type of autocratic management delegation. The Vice Presidents are actually *expeditors* with vice president titles. The titles are given to impress the customers, vendors and the finance world. *Yet, it is delegation.* It is at one end of the spectrum. The other end that says: "Do it the way I tell you and I will tell what you need to know." It is one way for the CEO, or President, to leverage himself.

The second point is that it works, and although it would not be a style that could be easily copied, even it you wanted to, it does work for some companies. More companies than you would like to believe started this way, and many are still being managed essentially by this management style.

The next example is one I saw first hand, from the beginning:

> The company is a successful communications company that has been on NASDAQ for seven years, growing at about fifteen percent per year, except in the last eighteen months it has lost considerable market share to its two main competitors. Executive management believes they have identified the problem as lack of commitment by the middle management. "The project managers are just not grabbing the ball and running with it.
>
> Executive Management's solution was to delegate more authority to the lower management and put the projects completely in the hands of the operations management. What was needed is to *empower* lower management

to achieve and excel by giving them the responsibility and authority to make it happen. This would be delegation of the highest order. To make it work, budget control was relaxed and expenditure authorization was put into the hands of the project managers. This was delegation the way some experts would like to see it - near total cutting loose and letting go. Only the broadest parameters were set out by executive management. This is at the end of the spectrum and says.

"I don't care how you do it; here is the money, now go make it happen."

In five months things began to happen. Progress was being reported in all three projects. The project managers were on their own and reported status at their option. Two months later disturbing news began to reach executive management who, up then, were patting themselves on the back for their bold act of empowerment. Two of the projects had budget overruns of nearly 200 percent. The third project was slightly over budget but ahead of schedule. However, this team had made long-term vendor commitments that would cost the company dearly for several years to come.

Normally, the executive management has tight controls over long-term financial commitments but under the "cut loose" delegation program, the teams were free to make almost any deal that would ensure success. Mandatory reporting to executive management was dropped to ensure that the delegation was complete and would not appear to have strings attached. The two other project managers had no idea how much over budget they had gone but when confronted with the facts, they felt their schedule achievements were justification for the over-runs.

In this case, the delegation went terribly wrong. The damage was more than the dollar amount involved. The long-term effect would be for the company to clamp down on delegation. That would hamper the company far into the future. The mistake by the executive management is that they failed to recognize that all the project managers and teams are not equal in their ability to juggle bottom line controls budgets and schedule priorities. They all needed guidance and close supervision in the areas in which they were weak or inexperienced. Management had failed to carefully discriminate and hold back the elements of delegation that would likely be mishandled.

BEFORE YOU DELEGATE, THINK ABOUT IT

Management needs to know several important things before they delegate, like:

Capability, experience and capacity of the delegate

The real doable schedule or goal

A clear understanding of the mission, schedules and issues

How much authority will be allowed and the parameters

Clear financial parameters and restrictions

Reporting duties and chain of command

HOW BADLY DO I WANT TO BE A DELEGATE?

Much has been written about the person who delegates, but too little has been said about the delegate, the person or persons upon whom the responsibility for the mission has been placed. You may become a delegate at any level of management. Even if you are the president of the company, your Board of Directors may delegate to you - now you are on the other end of the stick. If you have been offered a delegation, you need to take stock of what the assignment is and what the rules are going to be. Questions need to be asked like:

Who is my boss?
What is the assignment, precisely?
What is my authority?
How does the management measure success?
How does management measure failure?
What are the progress benchmarks?
What is the budget?
Are there any dependent factors?
What are the authority boundaries?
How much autonomy do I have?
Do I have the resources to pull it off?
What happens after the assignment?

These and other questions need to be asked and if possible, answered. Not all bosses will or can answer all these questions, but they should be asked anyway. If you have a responsible boss he or she will try to answer all your questions or find out the answers. Most bosses will likely be impressed by your grasp of the situation and the methodical way you trying to find out the parameters of the assignment. On the other hand if you have a boss that is irritated by your questions and feels you should be happy to be considered for the assignment at all, you may have a problem. These kinds of bosses may be unloading the assignment and will not likely be tied down to give real answers. We can expect that if the project is a success, he or she will take the most of the credit, and if it is a failure, he or she will be leading the headhunters.

THE DELEGATION MYTH

It is a wise manager who knows how, to whom and when to delegate, and a wiser person who can reject a delegation.

MOTIVATION, THE INSPIRATION OF THE UNINSPIRED

HERE I AM – MOTIVATE ME

Countless millions of dollars are spent on motivation schemes, programs and training. The idea seems to be that people will work harder, be more loyal, and be more productive if they are motivated. The problem is that it doesn't really work that way. I firmly believe that most desirable employees are motivated by opportunity, fair wages, reasonable working conditions, advancement opportunities and occasional sense of accomplishment. The ones that are not motivated by a fair amount of the above are not likely be motivated in any case. Highly motivated people seldom require all the goodies because they come motivated. In fact, motivated people are often satisfied with the opportunity just to make things work, make things better, to make things happen, and often in spite of the lack of rewards or niceties in their work life.

The other problem is that the motivation process is usually not transparent to those you are trying to motivate. That can make the process less sincere and even tacky. Most people know when they are being motivated and particularly if the process is not a clean process. The best motivational processes are out in the open where people can see it like a promotion for performance or a bonus given right after a new order is won.

My prime objective is to find, hire and keep motivated people. People too easily motivated are just as easily de-motivated. The secret is – **to find motivated people and keep them motivated.**

Trying to motivate people who will not be motivated is wasting your time. You are working on the wrong problem and the wrong people. Trying to motivate a cynic would be like trying to cure a confirmed drug addict by giving him a stern lecture. It may be possible to do so but you are likely to fail in the end.

De-motivation is the real danger for managers and executives. It is so easy to have a well-meaning motivation effort come off wrong, which does just the opposite of that intended. The de-motivation trap is out there waiting to happen to all of us.

THE PARETO THEORY TURNED ON ITS HEAD

The Pareto Theory is an idea that says; in many companies there are only 20% of the people doing 80% of the work. This is a novel and quaint concept, and in my opinion it is incorrectly applied here, and not even close to depicting what goes on in most businesses. Further, any business where 80 percent of the people are not pulling their share of the load is headed for the corporate landfill.

MOST COMPANIES HAVE MOTIVATED PEOPLE

Most enterprises are just the opposite where 80% are making chips fly and the 20% are lost souls. Where the opportunities are is when there are 50% doers and 50% watchers. Here we have the makings of a real opportunity to turn that company around - but not by wiping out the 50% watchers. What is usually needed is new management and leadership. The majority of those non-productive people are usually victims of poor systems, lack of systems, poor procedures and faulty or no real leadership.

The Pareto Theory is particularly erroneous about small start-up companies. There, anyone not pulling his or her load sticks out like a two-headed cow. There is no place to hide and the contributions are measured by everyone from the CEO right down to the fellow employee. Kangaroo courts are formed at the first sign of a shirker in their midst. The performers will not idly stand by while being impeded on their journey to the winner's circle.

Another reason why the Pareto theory is not generally correct is that in small to medium enterprises, smooth operations and progress are often accomplished by functional related environments where everything is connected, like in an assembly line. When one of the interconnected functions falls behind or fails, everyone knows, and they soon know why.

Perhaps the Pareto theory is more applicable to companies that are dysfunctional and will soon implode. These companies are seldom salvageable without a complete overhaul - starting at the top.

SLOGANS, POSTERS, INSPIRATIONAL MESSAGES AND OTHER MORAL BUILDERS

The money, time and management resources that are spent on motivation and morale building is enormous. When you think about it, some of these gimmicks are really compensation for inadequate management. If a company has poor morale, it is not likely to be improved by posters and slogans. The way to improve moral is to find and correct what is causing it. What is causing poor moral is not going to go away because of posters or a series of team building messages from the Personal or Human Relations Department. In my opinion, these devises actually do more harm than good. They can become disingenuous gestures of management when the real issues are not addressed.

Morale is difficult attain and keep at a high level, especially in companies that are performing poorly. But it is most difficult to build and maintain morale when there are cynics involved. In fact cynics are clear and present danger to the morale of any company. Cynics need very little reason to spread dissatisfaction and discord. These people have to go.

Having said that, we have to be sure that there are no other issues that need correction. If the issues are real, or perceived to be real, you can be sure that morale will continue degrade even after the cynics are gone. Real issues need to be attacked without prejudice. Real problems often go unearthed because someone or a group is protecting their turf or interests. There are so many reasons for poor morale that it would be impossible to mention all of them. However, we can talk about some of the most frequent offenders.

COMPENSATION

Compensation is often the reason for low morale, but it isn't always the dollar amount that is the problem. Often it is the way compensation is presented or administered. If the wage and salaries policies are not clear and understood, dissatisfaction is likely even if the compensation is actually more than fare.

MANAGEMENT DETACHMENT

Management detachment and aloofness is also a contributor to low morale. As much as possible management and the workers should be seen as partners with each having different roles. A management that appears to look down on their employees will pay for that arrogant posture. That kind of management can not really understand the employees and their needs. They need to go down on the production floor or out in the office floor, sit down next to Sally and say. "Sally, I really like the work you are doing. Tell me how you do it so well." Or words to that effect. Of course, management needs to be sincere. The must want to know their employees.

BAD MANAGEMENT

One bad manager or executive can sour a workforce. If a manager can not handle his or her authority, he or she needs to be apprised of the problem and if immediate improvement is not seen, they need to go. If upper management does not take action concerning a bad manager, then the company leadership becomes the real problem.

COMMUNICATIONS

Communication is essential to keep misinformation from getting started. Management needs to share information with the employees even if the information is not good news. There will always be rumors, but a company in trouble will have an abundance of rumors foretelling the worst to come. Management needs to be aware of what is happening in their company and they need to respond to rumors and issues that will affect morale.

NOTHING LIKE SUCCESS

The most powerful tool to insure high morale is success. When a company succeeds, everyone gets a piece of the action. Management's role can bring success. No one else can do it. The stockholders can not do it. The employees can not do it alone. Success can only be achieved by a management that continuously endeavors to improve all the elements of the company. On the other hand success is often responsible for lost momentum. People tend to take a pause and enjoy their success. Unless the management is swift enough to see this coming, they often get caught up in the celebrating and self-congratulations.

BE CAREFUL WHO YOU EMPOWER
YOU BOTH MAY BE LOOKING FOR A JOB.

Much has been written and said about empowerment, which should mean, "To enable, to give power, grant, to authorize and so on. It is likely that people who say they empower are really not doing it correctly or completely. The key is the denotation of the word "**give**". Very few managers or executives will willingly **give** away their authority or even lend it for a short time. It is more like the president talking to his staff of Vice Presidents saying:

> "I run a democratic company. You seven Vice presidents each have a vote on the decisions we make. Just remember, I have eight votes."

In times past we used words like: assign, appoint, commission, entrust, delegate, authorize, induct and so on. These words have specific meaning and implied limitations but the word empower is nearly limitless in the degrees of freedom implied. The point is: how many people actually give it all, pull the plug, and go the distance when they empower?

Empower is a word I dislike because it smacks of disingenuousness. It is something I would rarely do, as I believe few people would do either. It is a buzzword that can impress some people, unless they are inclined to look beyond the connotation and remember that people rarely give up power and control. Indeed, they usually seek more.

Chapter VII

THE QUALITY GAME

The reality is that many CEO's and executives do not know what to do with the quality effort in their company. The reason for this is that most top executives do not have a personal experience inside a quality organization. They are fearful of tampering with a function they know little about and could be blamed for some future quality mishap. Also some executives have had unpleasant or unsatisfactory relations with a quality effort and that left negative impressions about the role and value of quality organizations.

WHAT TO DO, OH WHAT TO DO?

Finding a useful role for the quality function should not be driven by custom or presumed purpose or automatically transplanted from previous experiences. The chances are if we are honest about it, much of our past quality experiences were not that great - unless you were lucky to be blessed with an enlightened quality organization.

THE QUALITY ROLE SHOULD BE DESIGNED TO COMPLEMENT AND ENHANCE THE PURPOSE AND THE EFFORT OF THE ENTERPRISE.

That means that the purpose of a quality organization must be thought through and specific goals set out that complement the grand plan of the enterprise. This is true if you are in a startup situation or contemplating improving the effectiveness of an existing quality organization. It is not enough to say that we want high quality products or Zero Defects or Total Quality Control. There must be a transition from slogans and banners and hype to functional systems. You have to design it and then integrate it into the culture of the company. Also, you cannot be vague or unclear about what quality is or how it will be measured. This is where many quality efforts go wrong. Too often executive management will hire a professional quality manager and leave it to him or her to take care of the details of design and implementation. The result is most likely a repeat of that manager's past experiences whether or not it is right for this company. More often than not, this is a serious mistake. There should be no management cop out. They must be involved and fully understand how the quality effort will complement and further the progress of the enterprise.

THE EVOLUTION OF THE CONCEPT OF QUALITY

Over the years my concept of quality organizations, and what they were supposed to do have changed radically. Having grown up in an industrial environment, I naturally emulated what my experiences had taught me in the early years of my career. My thoughts on Quality were also shaped by my roles in Quality Engineering and Quality Management in the very earliest years of my career. In those formative years I came to realize how ineffective and confined the quality effort could be. And, through the years I have seen and experienced so many ineffective and impotent quality organizations.

THE PERFECT QUALITY ORGANIZATION AND ROLE

It wasn't until years later when I had the opportunity to design my own organizations that I really began to question much of what I knew, or thought I knew, about the quality role. What has always interested me was the *function and responsibility* quality organizations should take, and not necessarily the conventional role or that traditional role that has permeated the business world in the past four decades - and continues much the same today.

Each time I did a startup or took over a company or operation, I changed or modified the quality organization to more investigating, intelligence gathering, enabling, teaching, defining and fact finding roles. Each time, I was motivated by the disturbing sense of inadequacy of mine and other quality organizations I observed. Each time I felt that I was getting closer to a more ideal role for quality - but no cigar yet.

The truth is I was not satisfied that I had designed the best possible quality organization and how it functioned in the company. Looking around, I was not impressed with other organizations either. Somewhere along the way I began to realize that the perfect quality role and organization I had been chasing did not exist, but I could come much closer than I have ever before – just keep trying.

THE QUALITY ROLE EVOLVES ALSO

Each company is unique and at each point in its. development, the needs change. I now believe that there are different quality roles for different phases of the company evolution. They may not be radically different but as the company moves ahead, so should the quality organization change in order to better serve the enterprise. For instance, in a young company, like a startup, the quality effort is likely to be more direct and involved in the day-to-day operations, like in the main effort of manufacturing. As the company develops and grows there should be a planned quality withdrawal and handing over inspection and audit to manufacturing.

CONFINED BY TRADITION

Historically, the quality function and role has been much too narrow and confined. This has reinforced a stereotype image that has not served the purpose of the enterprise well, and certainly has not portrayed the quality role as one of the supporting pillars of the enterprise. In many companies the quality organization has been relegated to near last in the pecking order with functions such as Marketing, Sales, Manufacturing and Engineering dominating the company power structure. In the less prominent role, it is difficult to address the broad quality needs of the company. Where quality issues need to be asserted, a full voice in the management of the company is essential.

WE LIKE IT THE WAY IT WAS

A common problem is that quality management often becomes more rigid, more entrenched, and more set in its ways as time goes on. Part of the reason comes from being on the defensive too often. In some companies the quality organization is the first to be blamed when a quality problem occurs. They are expected to catch all the mistakes other organizations make.

This is the result of a narrow and superficial understanding of the responsibilities of the different functions in the company. Unless there is guidance and perspective given by the company leadership, the quality organization can become an impediment to the success of the company. We talk about the need for innovation and progressive thinking from the company leadership but little is said about the need for organizational innovation for the quality effort.

THE IMAGE

An important aspect in the design of the quality organization is to achieve balance and as much as possible realize a sense of worth and value for the quality contribution. What plagues many quality organizations is their image. They are often seen as line stoppers, nitpickers and obstructionists, and some are, but it doesn't have to be that way. To avoid or change a bad image takes some functional strategy and very often surgery. We need to seek out ways to enable the quality effort to contribute to the overall effort in important, meaningful and less obvious ways.

WE ARE THE GUARDIANS OF QUALITY

It is also important that the quality image is not distorted by an exaggerated moral superiority. Sometimes the quality people seem to have taken the company high moral ground and stand as the undisputed authority of quality. They seem to be saying "WALK LOFTY AND CARRY A BIG STICK." They can give the impression that they have the license about the true meaning of quality and are the principle judge and jury of quality issues. This in no way pleases other parts of the company who have staked their own territory.

For instance, the engineers say they designed the product so they know more about how it functions and its limitations than anyone else. And the manufacturing people say they built the product and know every part and how it fits together. And, Marketing says they know the customer and what they need better than anyone else. . . . So, what is this moral quality high ground that some quality organizations think they own? The truth is that every part of the company has a stake in the quality business. There is nothing sacred about the business of defining and producing quality throughout the company.

THE QUALITY POWER STRUCTURE

Some Quality organizations go to extremes to obtain and maintain a credible and independent status with as much authority as possible. They are sometimes reporting to the President or CEO as a means to bolster their legitimacy, both inside the company and with the customers. However, it is more important that the quality effort have the wholehearted support of the upper management than any status on the organization chart. In some organizations, power may be the way to survive but whether a position of power aids a more effective quality function or better serves the enterprise is questionable. The real question is, what quality role can help produce the best products, lowest cost and with the highest customer satisfaction?

If the organizational structure of a company is such that the quality management is represented at the senior executive level because it is more effective there, then that makes sense. Yet in many companies the organization chart shows quality at the executive or upper management level. However, when major decisions are debated, the quality organization is not fully represented or is expected to keep a low profile the quality effort is compromised. An organization chart or a title does not guarantee management's commitment to quality effort. I have often seen quality management seated at the round table and their role was to be seen but not heard.

THE CONTRIBUTION

In order to prevent or change a bad quality image, there has to be value added by the contribution of the quality organization. If the role is primarily a policing function and little else, two things are usually true. The rest of the company will see the quality effort in a negative light, and therefore the bad image is generated. The other is that the quality organization itself will not have a sense of worth, pride and sharing in the contributions to the company effort. These two factors are bad enough but the overall damage is that the total effort and mission of the company is likely to be impeded or diminished because the quality organization is caught up in chasing defects and bad quality.

FROM WHAT TO WHY

Historically, many quality organizations have been focused on the *what,* and very little on the *why*. Much of the quality effort has been the finding or identifying quality problems and leaving the job of finding out *why* to others. I am convinced that quality organizations need to be involved in finding out why problems happen, and in many cases, helping to fix them. Otherwise, prevention may not have a dedicated and capable champion.

Finding out why is paramount to preventing future problems and installing safeguards that will arrest the problems in their early stages. Finding out why may take the quality effort into less traditional areas and to the far reaches of the organization. This is good for the company and for the quality effort. The quality effort needs to be operating in nearly all parts of the company.

THE STATISTICAL GAME MISUSED

Everything that happens has a reason. In the statistical quality game there is a distinction between causal defects and random defects. Causal defects are acted upon while random defects can often considered statistical random facts that occur in nature. The truth is that nothing happens without a reason and that reason needs to be identified.

Quality organizations often stop half way in the game and miss the opportunity to provide substantial contributions. They need to participate in finding out why, and go help fix the problems.

A good example was a computer device of extreme complexity that had a long history of 3% to 5% defectives. Just lowering the defect rate by 1% or 2% would save millions of dollars in product failures and extensive rework and re-inspection efforts, not to mention improving customer dissatisfaction. Quality management proposed a seven-point program to reduce the defects to 2% by close cooperation with five key vendors who supplied parts. At first management was cool on the plan because they believed the defect rate had been driven down to an optimum level and what defects remained were random. (This was the party-line from the previous quality management.) Therefore, continued effort to drive it lower would likely be futile - a waste of time and money.

A persistent quality management convinced the executive management to go ahead but the quality organization had to guarantee a minimum improvement of 1 1/2% in six months. They stuck their necks out because they firmly believed the problem was complacency and a convention of old ideas that were holding back progress. In three months the defects fell to just under 1%. In eight months the defect rate had fallen to 0.65%. In over two years the savings exceeded two and one half million dollars - in that company, it was a lot of money.

THE ADDED VALUE

Every company is different, even those that produce the same products or services. So, specific organizational design is not practical here. What I can address is the design of value producing quality functions so that real value is produced by the quality organization and their contributions are seen and appreciated by everyone in the company, as well as by the customers.

An example is to design the system so that quality is the responsibility of the people who built the product or provide the service. This is not new but it is a better way of assigning responsibility to the people who have the primary responsibility of building the product. The greater quality role should be to help define the meaning of quality, interpretation of quality and translating that into workable instructions, guidelines and systems to build the products or provide services. Also, they need to provide the means to measure what has happened, what is happening and to develop a system to provide reliable insight into future happenings. Quality science has many tools that can be designed and taught to all parts of the company. These are valuable tools that can help improve quality and cost.

Another worthy quality role is working with Marketing to understand what is it exactly that the customer wants; even if the customer doesn't seem to know. This can mean designing feedback systems for information gathering, but most of all obtaining the trust of customers so that there can be candid and open discussions that provide the means for long term customer satisfaction. Another tool is developing and maintaining statistics that help discover problem areas, real time, and identify cost saving opportunities.

Vendors and Suppliers are your Lifeline and Passport to Success.

TO THE SOURCE – TO THE SOURCE

Another lesson I learned was that the further you push quality back to the elements of your product or service, the more opportunity you have to control and improve it. In manufacturing, it means pushing quality back to the vendors, and to their vendors and to their vendors as far back as you can go.

Many conventional Quality people are confined to the classical quality arena within the enterprise, but the real game is out there where the materials, the parts, services, supplies and systems are made and provided. That is where much of the war should be waged. Solving problems and improving quality before the problems are in your house. It is a lot better then scrambling to fix them when they have infiltrated your company.

In one company we purchased over 85% of the product from vendors from all over the world. It was clear that we needed to concentrate on Making Vendors Successful. Much of what the company was doing was associated with vendors but it was not enough. We felt that we needed a combined force that had the professional skills to be able to understand the vendors' strengths and their weaknesses.

THE VENDOR SUPPORT GROUPS

The tool we devised was an organizational group with names like: **Vendor Engineering Support Teams and Vendor Engineering Teams.** The vendor groups usually consisted of a manufacturing engineer, a senior procurement person and a senior quality person. In one company we had seven groups and each group had three to five key vendors to work with. Close tracking of the vendor's performance was the basis for each groups focus and effort. Detailed, accurate and current information databases were designed by the quality group as a basis for measuring vendor performance and to develop an insight into the actions required. Each group was ranked on how well their assigned vendors improved.

The primary purpose of each group was to improve their assigned vendors performance in the areas of quality, on-time delivery, and cost, but cost was not the driving force behind this effort. We believed that if quality and on time delivery were the primary focus, lower cost would follow. Each fiscal quarter the group performance was measured and reported. New priorities were assigned, sometimes by the groups themselves and the activity of these groups was monitored regularly by the executive staff and the CEO. At times, the vendor quality groups encountered higher-level issues like this one in Singapore. A vendor had been producing machined castings on a model that was about to be phased out. They had been a very good vendor meeting cost on schedule deliveries, but their quality was just above marginal. The problem was their aging machinery. This meant that unless they could make a major upgrade in their machinery, they would not be qualified on the next product.

The vendor quality group assigned to that vendor requested the assistance of the finance department to help the vendor company obtain the necessary finance. Our finance department arranged a meeting with the vendor and the vendor's bank. Our presence was a strong recommendation and the vendor's bank quickly provided the necessary loan. With our support, the machinery upgrade allowed us to retain a valuable vendor.

A FAILED VENDOR IS YOUR FAILURE ALSO

This type of quality activity is another example of charging the quality organization with the role of support for vendors and suppliers and providers. A vendor that fails to deliver a quality product is an expensive experience. Everyone losses when a vendor fails. Not everyone in management understands how much time and money it takes to replace and develop a good, reliable vendor. Developing a key vendor can represent tens of thousands of dollars of invested time, so when a vendor fails, it hits you right in the profit column. It could and has cost millions.

ENABLING PROACTIVE QUALITY EFFORTS

Instead of designing a classical quality incoming inspection, think about working with the vendor to improve quality inside his company and further, into his vendors companies. The mission is helping vendors succeed. The role could be to select key vendors and suppliers for one-on-one support by helping them analyze the vendor's operations, systems and procedures and finding out whatever else could be causing the vendor to flounder or fail. Sometimes the Vendor support groups would come up with a problem that they felt they were not qualified to help the vendor with. It could then request assistance from senior management. The result was bringing resources and knowledge to a vendor's problem that neither the vendor nor the Vendor Support Groups could handle by themselves.

CUSTOM QUALITY BY DESIGN

My experience of being involved in many startups has taught me to discard much of the classical and traditional quality baggage. Three things have become progressively clear. The first is that the quality roll and resultant organizations should be as varied as the circumstances demand. The circumstances can be the company mission, customer's requirements, strengths and weaknesses in the organization, and the culture established or that which is desired. Secondly, if the design and culture is left to the senior Quality person without strong guidance from top management, the result is likely to be whatever that person's experiences were in the past. Brave new concepts and un-classical methods are not likely. The third is that without a respected seat at the round table, quality effort will continue to be seen but not heard.

YOU MIGHT NEED A DIFFERENT QUALITY STAFF

It is also wise to consider the strengths and weaknesses of the total organization when designing the quality role. That also means the selection of key people with skills and backgrounds to complement the desired quality role. This does not always mean the exclusive hiring of classical quality people - even the best you can find. Depending on the organizational strengths and weakness, the issues and the ongoing strategy, it may be necessary to hire people with special skills like engineering finance people, even legal people. It may be necessary to break the classical quality mold.

HERE CHANGE CAN BE GOOD

I came to the conclusion that the quality mission needs to be changing as the company changes and grows. These changes need not be intrusive or overly bold because major changes are often met with skepticism. For instance, if the company is competing in an industry that expects traditional organizational structures, it may not be wise to design what appears to be a totally foreign quality organization. But, the internal duties and interfacing with company functions can be as inventive and creative as the management can devise. As opportunities arise and problems surface, the company needs to be as flexible as possible. Traditional quality functions should not necessarily be employed just because they are traditional. There are so many ways to balance the efforts of the company effort. But, that is not likely to happen if the design of the company functions is based on stereotype design.

QUALITY SERVICES ARE NOT UNLIKE QUALITY PRODUCTS

In the service sector the quality role can mean defining what the customer wants and needs and knowing what he is getting - real time. What is quality service anyway? This can mean anticipating the customers ever changing needs by providing it even before the customer asks for or demands it. Defining what pristine service is and providing a practical measurement is a worthy task for any quality organization.

WHAT IS QUALITY ANYWAY?

I have listened to and read many definitions of quality. It reminds me of the continuing effort to define leadership. It likely can't be done, at least in a way that would satisfy most of us. However, I will give you the broad definition that I have used over the years:

> "A Quality product or service exceeds all of the parameters it was designed for and such design fully satisfies the intent of the product or service."

Sounds simple but it is saying a great deal when you consider "all of the parameters".

A common weakness in many organizations is defining what quality is. Even if the customer or engineering attempts to define quality, the definitions must be translated into usable and workable tools that can be implemented and the effectiveness of that implementation measured and tracked. The quality organization can be a strong influence in the definitions of quality that are continently changing.

PROMISES, PROMISES, PROMISES

We know quality by many monikers or labels, such as Total Quality Management, (Whatever that means), Quality Control (A contradiction in terms) and Quality Assurance (A questionable promise), to name a few. Although there are different names, the organizations and practices are remarkably similar. They usually organize to control rather than examine, counsel and resolve.

I can understand this because I spent a portion of my early industrial career in the quality business. I can remember that my job and the responsibility weighed heavenly on my young shoulders. I knew that if my efforts were to falter, or my authority was to be diminished, the company would surely fail. Actually, my job was not just a job; it was more like a religion. I knew that not all my fellow company workers and the management looked at the quality organization as I did, but I forgave them for they knew not what I knew - how could they?

BALANCE AND GOOD JUDGMENT

Executive management often fails to recognize areas of imbalance and the understanding of the changing values and priorities of the company. This is called: going asleep at the switch.

Quality management sometimes lose their way on difficult issues and complex problems as do other operations. A wise and proactive management should quickly intervene and counsel the quality operation when it losses its sense of balance and priorities. But, as mentioned earlier, management is less likely to intervene into quality business because they rarely have quality experience, that is, until the company is adversely affected.

IMAGE

Quality organizations run the gambit from credible and somewhat helpful to dismal failures that the company itself can't really do much about. There are many reasons for these failures but the most common is top management not stepping up and taking an active leadership role in the design and implementation of the quality effort.

EXPORTING QUALITY MANAGEMENT STYLE
WE GOT A LOT OF NERVE

Much of our Quality management systems do not work well in other countries unless they are modified and fine-tuned to fit that countries' culture. The sad truth is that they don't work that well here either. On paper, these foreign quality organizations look the same as those in the USA, but the way they work is different in every country.

WHO IS RESPONSIBLE FOR QUALITY?

Quality is always somebody else's problem. This is never more obvious than when CEOs and presidents can't be bothered with the quality issue so they assign it to someone in the organization to make sure they don't have to deal with it – until the customers start complaining about poor quality.

Often, the CEO or president does not have a quality engineering or quality management background which makes for less assertive management of the quality effort. They tend to avoid giving specific direction and in-depth questioning on exactly how, in detail, the quality effort will work. However, when things do go wrong, the most common solution is to replace the head of the quality organization. A successful quality program is born in the mind and actions of top management. It will not flourish long without their constant attention and support.

INSPECTION, THE WHIPPING BOY

In many companies inspection has been and still is the essential tool of the quality effort but not for the reasons many people think. It is not unusual to hear negative comments about the effectiveness of inspection. The problem is not inspection; it is the intent of the inspection process.

Inspection has been around, in more or less its preset form, for half a century or since WWII and in one form or another throughout recorded history. Actually, inspection can be traced back to ancient history where the practice was effectively employed.

Over the years industry has reshaped the inspection process but the results are about the same, and that was - to catch the defective, whatever's. Some companies view inspection as a cost center necessary to achieve the targeted quality level desired, and of course there is an inspection solution to achieve it. This is not good because it becomes an operation itself.

However, over time, inspection was hijacked and *Screening* became the method of achieving desired quality in many companies - it was a poor substitute. Inspection is a great and indispensable process to know and understand what is going on. The problem is, in some companies, inspection has become more of a tool to weed out defective parts than a scientific investigative process to identify, track down and solve problems.

THERE ARE VIRTUALLY NO RANDOM SOURCES OF SIGNIFICANT DEFECTIVES, BECAUSE THERE IS A REASON FOR EVERYTHING THAT HAPPENS.

Statistics can help us understand probabilities and other mathematical anomalies, but it can also lead us to accept the statistical probability. This is the premise for many statistical quality systems.

THE PROBLEM IS THAT STATISTICAL INTERPRETATIONS OFTEN FOCUS ON PROBABILITIES INSTEAD OF POSSIBILITIES.

Inspection should almost never be a screening process - as the policy or practice, as it deadens the company's sensitivity to defects that need not occur. Screening is like a anesthesia. If the targeted defective level is achieved, management can become complacent and secure in the thought that they are on target and that targeted defective level is at an acceptable level.

Continuous improvement of the process, product or service is essential for survival.

IT COMES DOWN TO THIS

There are very successful quality programs that are well respected inside the company and by the customers. There are, however, far too many companies that are stuck in an antiquated mind-set about the purpose and function of their quality effort.

The fault lies squarely in the lap of upper management. You would not think of telling your engineering department to go design something *good*, or instruct your human relations department to keep our employees *happy*. Yet, many quality organizations get little more direction than that or "Give us Zero Defects" or "We don't want to hear about quality problems from our customers."

The classical problems with quality programs go to the core of the company management mentality. If top management tolerates the quality function instead of embracing and guiding it, no position on the organization chart will make it work effectively.

Chapter VIII

MEETINGS MADNESS

Meetings promote indecision, delay, procrastination and are convient when are not sure about what we want to happen

Perhaps the most oblivious and most practiced form of Kicking Mice is the holding of meetings. Meetings are an abominable, primeval legacy, as basic as fear and sex. So much has been written about meetings, and the majority of is negative. Yet, meetings continue to consume an inordinate percentage of the workday. I am one of the many managers and executives that have wondered: How can we reduce the number of meetings while insuring that essential information is not sacrificed?

We often consider meetings as a normal and necessary process of doing business. It is, but only if it adds to process of the enterprise... The problem is that much of the meeting madness actually detracts from the enterprise efforts. The basic problem is that meetings are part of the way most animals function - *they flock.*

There are many reasons for excessive meetings; some are inherent in larger companies because they most likely did not develop effective communication tools as they grew. Another reason might be as the company grew, additional employees were hired who brought with them habits and management styles that embraced the meeting ritual.

THE FLOCKING SYNDROME
ANOTHER NAME FOR MEETINGS

However, I feel the real reasons for many meetings are deeper than the conscious will of man. Consider this:

WE HAVE TO FLOCK

Meetings of small or large groups are often caused by the natural tendency for humans to flock. The most common reason for flocking is fear, but there are other reasons as well. People flock when they are happy, as in parties and calibrations, when they are sad, as in funerals, when we demonstrate to show our position or displeasure, and when victory is achieved, as in parades. We love to flock for many necessary and important reasons.

The *Flocking Syndrome* has many manifestations and meetings are just one of them. As mentioned previously, meetings are called for a variety of reasons, but it is not always true that the person calling the meeting knows the real reason why he or she is doing it. Several reasons exist for meetings at the conscious level but the real reason is most likely in the subconscious mind, hidden deep in our genes. We know sheep flock for protection, birds flock, and fish school (another term for flocking) and many other creatures flock when they are threatened. And, so do the company managers, engineers, and the executives who may have problems they need to share, with someone-anyone.

We cannot really blame our ancestors for wanting to flock. It must have been tough out there alone with a Saber-Tooth-Tiger between the Neanderthal and his cave where his family and friends were waiting.

HAND-ME-DOWN MANAGEMENT RITUALS

You can thank your past bosses, managers and mentors who passed on some good, and unknowingly, some bad habits. Calling meetings is at the top of my list of bad habits. While serving our apprenticeship in industry and business, we were continually being trained to conduct business by our superiors. Their styles, mannerisms, good and bad habits were passed on to us. We learned to conduct ourselves by the examples set by people we feared and admired. Old rituals, like the meeting process, were reinforced because everyone from the president right on down to the lowest level supervisor did it. The result is another generation of misled people who themselves pass on what they have learned, creating another generation of *Meeting Madness*.

SHARE THE BURDEN

Meetings should do something to aid the business process, but do they? Many meetings are called because the person calling the meeting has a problem and hopes to find a solution, or merely wants to share his or her burden. Or, they need to call a meeting because that is how it has always has been done. Most young managers cannot wait to call their first meeting (I know I did); it is a symbol of having reached some level of position and authority.

The classic example of how meetings happen is when the president or CEO chews out the staff for lack of performance or a shipment shortfall. At the end of the meeting the executive conference room door swings open and a stream of worried looking vice presidents and managers head for their offices. The first thing they do is to call in the secretary to schedule a meeting of his or her staff. Most will schedule that meeting the same day because they have to share or transfer the burden their boss had just given them. At the first sign of danger, the instinct is to flock.

Few managers are aware that they may be seeking protection in numbers when they call a meeting. He or she is a lot more confidant of meeting the threat or danger surrounded by their colleagues than alone in the office.

THE EGO TRIP

Then there are the managers and executives that call meetings because of the need to nourish their ego. This is the most difficult meeting to get through without exposing your disinterest and lack of reverence. This type of manager honestly believes these sermons are essential for your orientation and development. This type loves to hear themselves talk. To make it worse, the audience has learned that it is better to appear to be impressed and grateful than to be indifferent and contemptuous. The lectures are often followed by praise and flattery by individuals in the audience who feel the need to patronize the boss. This only encourages him or her to give more lectures – and they don't get better over time.

YOU CAN'T WAIT TO CALL YOUR FIRST MEETING

Sooner or later nearly everyone reaches the point where they have the prerogative to call meetings. My advice is, think before you do it. *One-on-one,* is often a much more effective method to inform, persuade, and influence others. Too many managers hide behind their office door or in the multitude of meeting attendees. Get out there and attack the problems or issues directly - *mono e mono.*

LONG MEETINGS - A BAD IDEA

Long meetings almost never work. Whatever good is passed on has to compete with the feeling of boredom, contempt, and disrespect for the speaker, speakers and the establishment in general. Most attendees soon wish they were somewhere else – even back at their desk tackling that stack of paperwork. There is nothing more annoying then having to drop what you are doing to attend a poorly organized meeting that didn't need to be called, and you didn't need to attend.

A MEETING CHECKLIST

When you are tempted to call a meeting, these are some questions that should be asked:

1. *Do I really know why I want to call this meeting?*
2. *Have I thought out alternative solutions to a meeting?*
3. *Will a meeting really solve this problem?*
4. *How can I do this without a meeting?*
5. *If I need to call a meeting, who absolutely needs to be there?*
6. *Do I have time to get my act together before the meeting?*
7. *Have I anticipated the questions and reaction?*
8. *How can I get this done in the shortest possible time?*

9. *Do I need to do some pre-meeting consultation and networking?*
10. *How can I get feedback on the meeting's effectiveness?*

If after questions like these have been asked and answered, and you still feel you need to call a meeting – do it. Chances are the meeting will be more productive having gone through a simple checklist.

DEFINITION OF A BAD MEETING

We have all experienced meetings that left something to be desired.

A bad meeting is one that:

Leaves people confused
Makes people wish they were somewhere else
Leaves people with the wrong message
Leaves people with no message
People feel was a waste of time
Raises more questions than it answers
Diminishes confidence in the management

And, should have never been called in the first place.

WHEN IS A MEETING NOT A MEETING?

I would like to make the distinction between meetings and work sessions. Much of the horsepower of a company is generated in properly organized work sessions. These can take the form of reviews of all kinds such as: status reviews, financial reviews, shipment reviews, engineering reviews, marketing reviews, over - views and planning sessions. These assemblies are organized and disciplined to status, track, and if necessary, provoke corrective action or some form of redirection. A properly designed and executed work session is usually characterized by much of the detail; and data being generated and assembled behind the scenes. This facilitates the group to quickly assess the state of affairs. I often use regular work sessions to build companies, and it is not unusual to status a complete project that has three to five hundred action items in thirty minutes - because the homework had been done before the meeting.

As previously stated, tracking the status and progress of programs, projects and other company business by work sessions is the very foundation of successful businesses. These sessions only resemble meetings because there is a gathering of people. What characterizes a work session is the preparation and organization that goes on behind the scenes, before the work sessions. These too can get out of hand if they are turned into the classical meeting scenario. The art of conducting a successful work session is not that different from conducting a meeting, except that the purpose is usually clear and specific. Unless the work sessions are kept sharp, interesting and actually serve the purpose for which they were created, they could become more like meetings.

YOU CAN MAKE EVEN A BAD MEETING COUNT

Although the great majority of meetings are a waste of time, it is impossible to avoid them. For those meetings you do attend, a special mindset could be helpful. Go into meetings with the determination to: contribute, guide, learn, and if appropriate, lead the group. Your enthusiasm can ignite an otherwise indifferent and non-productive group. You can make even a bad meeting count.

MEETINGS - A BAD PLACE TO SOLVE PROBLEMS

The purpose of meetings is usually to inform, solicit or collect information, but not usually to solve problems. Problems can be solved during the meeting process. However, even if that happens it is not normally the result of the meeting process. Usually, there are just a few people that are in a position to use the information to solve problems. To solve problems, you do not need, nor can you utilize most of the people that attend the meetings, and that includes the bystanders. Problem solving is best done outside of meetings.

MEETINGS CAN WORK

As with everything, there are exceptions. There are useful meetings that do powerful things for the organization. Meetings are a convenient way to make sure that the whole organization receives the same messages at the same time. It is also a way to report company business status and progress. Additionally, it can be a powerful media for handing out accolades and thanks for a job well done. However, I repeat, meetings are rarely a place to solve problems.

GOOD MEETINGS DON'T JUST HAPPEN

A good meeting comes off right because of the planning and work put in before it starts. The person calling the meeting needs to consider who really needs to be there. There needs to be an agenda, written and handed out or structured carefully in the mind. You need to decide what needs to happen or what the goal of the meeting is. It is also true that the meeting needs to be controlled. A firm hand is sometimes necessary to keep a meeting on track. The leader can be firm without being overbearing or dictatorial. The meeting needs to be short and crisp and when it is adjourned, someone needs to recap the meeting and what transpired. It should not drag on and on. Follow-up is essential. Someone needs to be assigned to follow-up on specific issues. Closure is necessary for a successful business process. The attendees should walk out of the meeting with the feeling that they accomplished something, but too few do. Most people feel that meetings are a waste of time and they are usually right. One study stated that out of a 40 hour work week, they spent 16-17 hours in meetings. More importantly, most poorly prepared meetings rarely accomplished anything.

BE SURE YOU KNOW WHY

There are many books on how to conduct meetings. I recommend anyone trying to improve their meeting skills read some of them. However, not many deal with the forces that provoke meetings. Here is where we all need to search our motives and consider possible alternatives. My recommendation is that there is a thorough review why the meeting needs to be called. If then it still seems necessary, then it should go ahead. If not, find another direct and personal way to inform, review or disseminate the message. But, if a leader really needs the support of others because the problems are mounting and feels the need to share the problems, I suggest that person get his or her act together or perhaps consider another profession.

Chapter IX

PARTICIPATIVE MANAGEMENT

Participative Management (PM) has been identified with the concept of having the worker level make the decisions on how they will carry out the company's tasks. These decisions are usually reserved for management. In my opinion, PM is an unsustainable management contrivance. It is more of a Japanese tool, but it has been exported all over the world. However, even today, long after PM was imported from Japan, most companies still manage with authoritative style.

The idea is that people will perform at higher levels if they have a say in what and how things are done. In theory it sounds right and like other socially attractive concepts, they often fail because of many reasons. I think we have seen the PM practice peak in the United States and in more recent years has lost some of its appeal.

We Americans have had forms of worker participation in management decisions for decades. Most progressive companies have regular meetings with their employees and worker input to management is often used to change or modify company procedures and the modus operandi However, in most companies the employee participation is out in the open and there is little pretense that management will act on every input just because they come from the workers. Some variations of PM that have developed are interesting, if not sometimes clandestine. Bottoms-up decision making is not new but there have been some interesting variations such as the one described below. I was privileged to see this in action, first hand.

The Scene is a meeting of the boss and his staff. The boss sits at the head of the table with his staff eagerly waiting for the leader to describe a particular production problem – production volume must be increased and the operating cost must come down. Management has worked out a detailed plan and has decided to implement the plan by having it appear to originate at the worker level. To do this management will help the process along with some PM Sessions.

This begins as a typical company meeting. The leader has called a meeting to motivate the workers in the direction management has chosen.

After throwing the problem out on the table, the leader sits back and listens to the workers as they attack the problem. A healthy debate ensues and the group seems to be moving in the right direction. The leader leans forward in his chair and shows intense interest, nodding approval from time to time. He also reinforces his body language approval with verbal comments like: "right!" and right on! "On occasion the leader will stand up, walk over the persons speaking and stand beside him or her as if in support for some point they were making. A mental note is made by everyone in the room, but not always in a conscious way. As the meeting progresses the group moves into an area that is not what the management wants to have happen. At this point the leader seems to lose interest and he pushes back from the table; his gaze wanders to the window. This too is noticed by the group, even though the leader is not directly involved in the discussion, his body language sends a clear message.

Leader's sudden disinterest and begins to change the direction of the discussion. Soon they are back on track and the leader is again a picture of intense interest. He is smiling, nodding and his body langue is a portrait of approval. Yet, throughout this process the leader has scarcely said a word except to ask for more detail on some favorable statement.

This process continues over several meetings with the group progressing, more or less in the direction that management has previously decided upon. The process is like a sailboat tacking back and forth, heading in the general intended direction, but not always pointed at the end objective. Once the group has set a course that management has decided upon, the leader can easily correct any small deviation in direction by simple body language or liberal interpretation of the group's findings.

Dose this work? Sometimes, but it works only a few times unless the participants learn to see the leader as a consular, advisor and teacher, and accept this form of PM as his or her style. The problem with this style of PM is that it is easily seen through if the leader is not very skilled at group leadership.

It is possible that some of the group will come to understand or suspect what is going on. If the leader is respected, and the course seems reasonable, even these more perceptive people will support the outcome.

The danger is that if the leader is not trusted, is disliked, or has a history of using people, the system will not work and the organization will be much worse off.

I have always felt that the some versions of PM verges on the edge of manipulation and therefore a risky undertaking at best. It has numerous aspects that contain opportunities for worker distrust and loss of respect for management. If you consider the questionable gains in productivity or efficiency verses the potential risks, it is an easy choice for me.

I could not use PM. In fact I would make a mess of it. And that is the problem with other management styles as well. To really work well, a management style needs to be second nature to the person leading the group of employees. Not only do you need to fully understand it and how to administer it, you need to understand its limitations. Management styles also need to have responsive and compatible environments. Not all styles work in all companies. So much depends on the background, personalities and capabilities of the people involved, both on the management side and also on the worker side.

It is just not my style. What does work is participation of workers in the process of decision - making where it is practical and the issues and solutions are within the purview of the workers.

THE JAPANESE PARTICIPATIVE MANAGEMENT

The manager's manager

It's amazing what can be done with the right press agents. People will believe just about anything. World Leaders, Politicians, Educators and Managers are no exception. A popular Myth is that the Japanese possess superior management skills. It is not clear who created this image but many American and Japanese executives believe it. I do not believe it. What I do believe is that they have capitalized on their own cataclysmic defeat in WW II, and the naivety and the generosity of a benevolent victor.

Consider this: Just after World War II, the time was right, the culture was ready, and the American Government financed the entire Japanese venture - **Japan Incorporated**. We became the Venture Capitalist of all time. Japan became our biggest and most successful start-up. At the end of the 1950's the wheel of fortune came to rest on Japan. Germany, Hong Kong, Singapore, and Taiwan, but Japan and Germany were quick to grab the opportunity. Another key factor was that America was anxious to show the world how the Western Civilized Culture could handle victory with its democratized morality.

That was our contribution. The Japanese, on the other hand, had a lot going for them. Their culture is very structured with considerable governmental, civil and personal discipline. The big boost was starting over. Japan and Germany both enjoyed the advantages of building brand new industrial infrastructures. They both took advantage of retooling for increased efficiency and improved quality. All these factors made both Japan and Germany formidable competitors. I believe these factors more than superior management ability was responsible for their successes.

To our credit, Americans will try anything, even if we have no idea what the end result will turn out to be. When PM came along we were ready to give it a try. Other experimentations with management concepts have produced some successes, and more then a few stunning failures. Even with our, sometimes, veneer mentality, some of these systems seem to work - for a time. Some of these failures we know of, but most have been swept under the corporate rug. Some will argue that PM is not exclusively Japanese. However, Japan is the biggest PM showcase. Many American companies jumped on the PM bandwagon only to find it was not the panacea of management styles. It was not the motivation elixir for all American companies. What we failed to realize was that this tool was one of many Japanese management tools that came out of their management toolbox.

These individual tools rarely work well alone. They are part of the Japanese Management Tool Set – sort of like the tools in the Swiss Army Knife. Involved here is Japan's long-standing culture, and age old systems of worker/management relations.

We can give the Japanese their just dues, but I believe much of the mystique over their management abilities is not justified. Japan has its successes and failures like the US and other developed countries. We seem to attach a mystique to anything we do not understand, and we Americans are not very good at understanding other cultures. Some Americans believe if they read Buddha, a book on Feng Shui and Japanese Quality Circles, they will have mastered the Asian mind. We make a big thing about the smallest difference in culture styles and practices. Most of the time these differences have little to do with the real reasons for their success or failures.

It is a serious mistake to emulate the Japanese or anyone else believing their ideas will work wonders in our environment and culture. In fact, they may not be working that well where they came from. What works in Japan (and not forever, in any case) are systems that are connected to every thread of the Japanese social, moral, political and traditional fabric that is Japan. These systems are connected to all aspects of Japanese life that stretches back over thousands years. Taking a page from the book of Japanese Management is like taking one thread out of a tapestry and then trying to weave a duplicate.

I have considerable experience with Japanese management and I respect their abilities, but I do not fear to compete with them. The advantages in their style can sometimes be their weakness. I admire their attention to detail and their ability to take things to their most elementary levels. In contrast we Americans often slough over things and end up with a broad brush that spells trouble later.

Much criticism of authoritative management styles comes from the critics that claim the employees are not listened to. They have no way to communicate their ideas to management. I think this argument is very much exaggerated, especially with most US companies. Also my experience in developing countries is that there are many enlightened company managers that do provide ways for worker participation and open dialogue with their management. In high volume manufacturing environments the worker is trained to do a limited amount of operations. This has both advantages and disadvantages. The advantages are obvious, with fewer operations; the employee's time to train is shorter. Also, employee turnover is not as critical as it is when they loose a highly trained employee.

One disadvantage of high volume production environments is the employee often suffers from low job satisfaction. When this happens the employee is likely to look at his or her job as just a paycheck and company loyalty is minimal. Under these circumstances considerably more attention to the employee is necessary. There should be more group and company meetings aimed at improving the employee's awareness of the company's appreciation of the employee's efforts. The importance of the employees work should be stressed often.

IT WORKS IN SOME ENVIRONMENTS – BUT NOT ALL

I think PM tactics are of little help when the employee's functions are highly structured like in an assembly line where any change can impact many other operations. In this environment, employee's opportunities for implementing improvements are limited, but still possible. I made it a habit to walk the production line often in my factories. This is not just to show the employee's management's interest in their work but also it is an opportunity to interface with the production workers. I have received many valid suggestions this way. When some of these were actually acted upon, the contributor was always given credit for the contribution. Walking the line, out there with the workers, by upper management is also a good example for the lower management to follow.

What often happens is that suggestions in highly structured environments have less chance of being implemented than in lesser structured environments. Because of this, employees can become discouraged because management often fails to act upon their suggestions.

The conclusion I have reached is that PM is not helpful in most environments I have known. I think that is the key to the argument, that any management style needs to be tailored to the circumstances. That includes the people involved, the style of management, incentives and the culture of the company.

It is difficult to say one management style is preferred over another. What works best for me is a combination of management styles, or elements of several styles. I have been fortunate to have been exposed to many diverse management challenges. Most of the time I employed a management style of mine that has been most successful for me. Yet, there were times that required more mentoring, coaching and more teaching. Also, in a few cases, I have encountered a hostile environment that required drastic modification of my usual management style. Managing companies in the USA is different than in developing countries. Managing High technology companies is also different than, let's say, commodity companies. I believe the style best used is one that is derived by carefully assessing the state of the company and its employees.

Taking over developed companies requires special consideration. For several years of my career I was as a "company doctor", a term used to describe someone who is hired to fix **sick** companies. That job requires swift action to stop the red ink.

This means you need to quickly understand what has happened and you often have just a few days to find out who the bad guys are, and who good guys are. Older companies have established environments and ways of doing things. You have to quickly determine what to overturn and what to leave in place.

Management style often plays a big role in a troubled company and is often the reason for the company's dilemma.

Stepping in and taking over a troubled company is a traumatic event. Here, it is almost always requires a strong authoritative style. The employees are aware that the company is in trouble, so just about any style that works will be accepted. The fastest way to fix troubled companies problems is to have one experienced person at the top making the tough decisions. Democratic processes are slow and often indecisive. When a company is on the brink of failure, decisions must be made quickly and the required action must be swift and sure.

Chapter X

THE CHANGE SYNDROME

We are being bombarded with books, articles and endless rhetoric telling us that the business world is changing as never before. We are being told that we must change, and that those that do not change are surely lost.

What is the business world preaching about change? What do business gurus and high priests of enlightened management mean when they tell us we must change to meet the new millennium demands, the new dawn, the new world? What is all the new change mania about? Is someone trying to sell us a bill of goods or is the business world really spinning out of control?

First, consider this past century. In the past one hundred years the world changed beyond anyone's wildest imagination. If you don't consider pasteurization, the automobile, the airplane, computers, atomic energy, and space travel as significant agents of change, then nothing qualifies as change.

Change has been continuous, with periods of acceleration. Much of the accelerated changes are provoked by events such as war. The atomic bomb is the direct product of the WW II era and even though it was inevitable, the atomic age was catapulted into the twentieth century by the urgency of WW II. Even the threat of war has created or accelerated change. However, the worldwide changes we face today are largely due to the explosion of technology, communications and the threat of conflict.

So change is not new to us, it has been our constant companion since, and even before, recorded time. What is new about change is the *Rate of Change* or *delta* (Δ). Communications, speed of travel, information access, technology advances and other factors have revved up the action and reaction time of just about everything. Companies are struggling to keep up with the *speed* of change.

The problem for many companies is deciding what to change, what to change to, and the most difficult problem is how to execute change. Of course, progress requires change of some sort, so let's define change. Is it: Tweaking, improving, fixing, smoothing, streamlining, realigning, adjusting, resizing, shifting, correcting, modifying, molding, rearranging, or any other normal process of improvement?

No, not these kinds of change...The kind of change referred to by most students and promoters of change, and what I am referring to, can be described as somewhere between metamorphosis, major change, tergiversation and basic change. Examples of the kinds of change that fall into these definitions: opening up major sales operations in the European market having never before sold out side of the USA, or, for the first time, acquiring another company and folding it into your company, going from a basic manual "Order Processing System" to a completely "Computerized Automated System", or going from a classical autocratic, pyramid management structure to matrix management style. This would be change.

SELLING CHANGE AND GRASPING FOR STRAWS

Selling change today is easy as the economy soars and then falls to desperate depths. Change is easy to sell when your company has its back to the wall, and change is often perceived as the magic elixir for companies in trouble. The problem is that some of these companies do not need new concepts, ideas or new systems.

"They need to get it right"

Why do otherwise intelligent executives and managers keep looking for that shiny new management concept or novel management innovation? Actually, most systems and concepts are workable if people really want them to work, and if they are willing to systematically grind out the rough spots and hone it to a finely tuned tool. The fact is that there are thousands of different and successful systems, procedures, practices, policies and methods of operations that are different. The point is that most are successful. Every successful company is different, even between divisions of the same company where they strive to be identical.

I go as far to say that a somewhat inefficient system is better then something new and untried and not understood. An example was a visit to a Japanese company in Osaka that made precision components for computer disk drives. This was in the late 1990's when most high-tech companies had computers in every office, real time process control, and imbedded accounting reporting throughout the company.

The factory tour took me through the administration, and accounting offices where not one computer was to be seen.

And, out on the production floor not a single computer in sight. What I saw were manual adding machines, slide rules, and abbacies, everywhere. Now this company was the leading producer in the world for these very precise micro-miniature parts. They were successful and very profitable, and they were at least five years behind the West in automation and computer systems usage. Was this a strange paradox? Not really, because it is an example of *getting it right* rather then being seduced by the allure for change. There is no doubt that the company eventually moved into the world of automation and computers, but you can bet your last dollar that they did it with extreme caution, detailed planning and a precise focus on the overall priorities of the company. Fancy new business gimmicks or even more proven or efficient ways of doing business did not mesmerize them.

CHANGE – THE SLIPPERY DEVIL

It is difficult to explain how arduous it is to effect change. By that I mean to make it happen and endure – no mater how insignificant a change might seem to be. Some people act as if change is something you just decide to do, and you go out and make it happen. Not only is change difficult to do, but it is so slippery that before you know what is happening, whatever you changed often reverts back to where it was or to something worse then you had before.

"TO CHANGE OR NOT TO CHANGE, THAT IS THE QUESTION."

The most difficult management choice to make is to decide if you need to make a change in your strategy, your modus operandi, operations or plans. Should you first figure out exactly what you are not doing or what you are doing wrong? Most of the time you need to find out what you are doing; I mean really understand it in precise detail. There are too many managers and executives that go about making changes when they really do not know from what they are changing. Very often the understanding of their environment is superficial because these mangers and executives consider details of the business are someone else's concern. **Their focus is on the big picture.** They have delegated the task of in-depth understanding and the mechanics of how the company works to someone else, and so, understandably, these executives do not understand how the company really works anymore.

NO BREAD CRUMBS TO FIND YOUR WAY BACK

It is also common for management to lose their way when companies go through repeated changes of management, re-organization, resizing, and frequent product transitions. The people that knew why something was done and how it worked are no longer there. The new management often has only superficial understanding of what is going on under the surface.

An example of this management detour is a situation in a Silicon Valley company where I was called in to investigate the reasons for export/import irregularities causing delayed shipments and fines. It didn't take long to find out the root of the problem.

The people in shipping and receiving were in charge of imports/exports but they had never studied or were trained in the regulations and procedures of a very complex and important business process. Going back in time, the pieces fell into place.

The import/export management was once in the hands of people who were well trained and were constantly updated on the many changes in U.S. Custom and the offshore countries rules and regulations they worked with. As business declined and cutbacks ensued, the import/export department was downsized until just a few people remained. Recent management changes had resulted in an executive management that knew little about the mechanics of international business. They were brought in to stop the red ink any way they could.

When the new management took over, they went through every department and made drastic changes to cut costs. Eventually, the import/export department was so small that they decided to merge with shipping and receiving who, by the way, knew nothing of the technicalities of import/export procedures and regulations. Soon there were no people left who were experienced in customs procedures and the rules and regulations. The receiving/shipping responsibilities now included the customs functions that they knew little about.

Executive management had little understanding of the importance of knowing and following the customs rules, until tragic things began to happen. Shipments were held up because of improper paperwork. Incoming materials were impounded causing production lines to go down and fines were becoming frequent and expensive. Numerous fines were levied and the company was under close scrutiny by the customs organization. To add to the problem the developing countries they shipped materials to frequently held up delivery of much needed materials because the paperwork was incorrect.

Upper management blamed the problem on the manager and people in shipping/receiving because they did not understand the business they had inherited. Until the problem was identified, executive management was planning on making several personnel changes in that department. They believed that by changing the management of the shipping and receiving department, the problems would go away.

The review I conducted put the spotlight on having competent and knowledgeable management that understood customs and the need to continually educate and stay current with the ever-changing regulations. It also stressed that austerity measures in critical areas like import/export was foolhardy.

The remedy here was to reinstate the customs group with people trained to administer import/export business who would thereafter report to the Director of Marketing and although Marketing was, in this case, a good choice, other organizations could have been chosen also. What was important is that specially trained, knowledgeable people are required to administer this special part of the business. Making changes is the easy part. Living with the change can be difficult.

CHANGE APPEARS EASIER THAN FINDING THE REAL PROBLEM

Many companies are so caught up with the mania for change that they do not take the time to understand what they are doing and what they need to do to get it right. It often appears much easier to sweep aside what is in place, or what another organization did, than dig into it and find out what is really wrong. This is partly because there are problems that arise when you go forth with a real problem solving effort. Individuals as well as groups become defensive and protective. Otherwise cooperative people become evasive and vague. Some will point the finger at other individuals or groups, which increases the tension and mistrust among the troops. The other reason is that the ego of some managers and executives causes them to put their own stamp on the origination and change becomes much more personal. Although the path of least resistance is attractive, that is just change it, most often the situation would have been far better off by finding exactly what needs fixing then starting all over.

"HERE COMES DA JUDGE"

It is not uncommon to see a new CEO come on board and everyone holding their breath waiting for the changes that will surely come. Everyone expects the new CEO to make changes, and the most expectant are usually the Board of Directors that hired him or her. Most experienced leaders usually take the time to find out what is really wrong with the company and then surgically fix the problem(s). The overconfident and less secure often jump in and start whacking away. Swift action may be the right medicine for a few very sick companies, but not always.

RESISTERS OF CHANGE
Yes! I'm guilty.

Yes, I often resist change. I am one of those people they talk about, "**A RESISTER OF CHANGE.**" The reason I sometimes resist change is simple.

> *I don't believe some of the change masters*
> *know what they are doing.*

I have seen it far too often. A situation, most of the time improperly analyzed or inadequately defined, is diagnosed before the real problem can be ascertained. The prescription is invariably - **change it!**

STRANGERS IN THERE OWN COMPANY

It may come as a surprise to some that management's IQ about their company's details is often unacceptably low - as described here:

One company I worked with was contemplating moving their offshore manufacturing operations from one Asian country to another Asian country because they believed that the lower cost labor there would boost profits by significantly lowering overall costs. They were chasing cheap labor. They were also unhappy with the performance of their Southeast Asian operations because it was producing marginal profits. I was asked to evaluate several other country locations that I believed would be more profitable.

I decided that my first task was to find out everything I could about their offshore operations. I was not surprised to find that few at headquarters knew anything specific about how the offshore operations worked, and what kind of problems they were having. I asked to look at the communications for the last three months to see if there were obvious problems. There were considerable problems and they reappeared frequently, indicating to me that no one was listening. I decided to visit the operations in Singapore to see what was really going on. What I found was: delayed materials shipments from headquarters, shortages, unanswered inquiries and requests for help, requests for engineering changes ignored, late funds transfers and an inexperienced offshore Managing Director who did not know how to confront corporate headquarters to resolve the problems and obtain the required support.

Here we have a sick subsidiary and no one knew what was going on, but headquarters had decided that the operation would be better shut down and set up in a lower cost country. The management jumped to the common conclusion that **change** was the answer.

In this case, change was defeated in favor of fixing the problems by digging deep into the guts of the corporation's management failures of both headquarters and the offshore operations. Improvements in procedures, accountability, follow up, and a two man communications and support team in corporate headquarters was the right medicine in this case. With proper reporting and regular reviews the Singapore operation turned around in just four months. Confronted by the real status and the real problems, the management was willing to accept the responsibility for the status quo and eagerly supported the necessary reform. Unfortunately, the change masters often win the day by stampeding management into a change that has a good chance of failing, leaving the original problems still there, still unresolved and often more difficult then ever to fix.

CHANGE ETERNAL

What is changing? Yes, we are in a world that is changing. But, that has always been so. As previously stated, the important factor is the *Rate of Change or delta*. And, it is accelerating at an incredible rate, due mostly to communications and closer contact worldwide, or as some would put it - Globalization.

We know that change has been going on ever since the earliest times, but now the rate of change is on a fast track, but not necessarily always on a *new* track. Companies that have survived decade after decade of changes (and the world is full of them) did so because they continually coped with the rate of change. Companies that survive have learned how to keep up with the rate of change; they realized the need for a more nimble and responsive management.

CHANGE PANIC

The illusion is that we must do something, fast, or we will be run down, devoured, and destroyed. It is this illusion that we must do something fast that can panic naïve and desperate management. We have names for the future, like The New Frontier, The New Millennium, The Information Age, and many more brave new labels, all supposedly calling for change. We are meant to believe that these new labels describe a brave new and dangerous world that has arrived. And, if we don't do something, we will be left behind, mowed down and destroyed.

"Comes the revolution, everything will be different. It may not be better but it sure as hell will be different."

The hucksters of change are preaching that we must discard the past and embrace the future but they fail to mention we are a product of our past and we cannot discard it anymore then zebras can change their stripes.

THEY NEED TO GET IT RIGHT

Consider how ludicrous it is to prescribe change when management does not understand what they are doing now. And yet, that is precisely what happens in far too many change efforts. Most often, instead of change, **they need to get it right.**

To make an intelligent change you need to know what you are doing now, how you got there, what is wrong, and then decide on precisely what needs to be done. Most of all, a serious effort must be made to determine the collateral damage that is likely to occur if significant changes are introduced. And, then a plan and the execution must be played out with intense attention to detail. Effecting change, real and stable change, may be the most difficult thing you will attempt in today's business environment.

THE NATURE OF CHANGE

The nature of change is that it disturbs the status quo. Most people do not necessarily like the way things are, but even more, they dislike something new. Not all companies are the same but my guess is that employees usually fall into these categories:

- Twenty percent accept the change because they see the value and the future potential.
- Ten percent accept change because it could put them into good graces with the boss.
- Thirty percent are neither pro nor con. They don't care one way or the other.
- Another thirty percent are cynical about anything management does. It doesn't make any difference what it is, if management wants it, it must be bad.
- And finally ten percent are directly threatened by the change. No way do they want the change to succeed.

NOW, THAT IS A STACKED DECK

Any thought that persuasion, cajoling, or promises of good things to come will bring these people together is unrealistic.

BIG CHANGES OR LITTLE ONES – WHICH IS THE EASIEST

At one time in my career I thought change was like anything else, the more there is to deal with, the more difficult it is, and conversely, the smaller it is, the easier is will be. I had to learn the hard way.

I had just finished founding a new manufacturing subsidiary of several thousand employees when I was asked to build another, much smaller manufacturing arm in a nearby country. Having just successfully completed a large project, I was convinced that the same planning and attention to detail was not required for this rather small project. I delegated some tasks and oversight that I used to hold sacred.

It wasn't long before the project began to fall behind schedule and surprises began to crop up. At first I felt the people I had put in charge were falling down on the job, but after a careful investigation, I realized the fault lie with my planning. Normally I left no known detail to chance when planning a complex project. This time I mistakenly assumed the detail was obvious and the issues would be resolved routinely. My conclusion was that there is no middle ground when it comes to management of the details and even relatively simple projects or changes are almost equally difficult to implement.

CLEANING UP SOMEONE ELSE'S MESS

Cleaning up a mess is far more distasteful then scrapping it and starting over. I know from experience that it is a great temptation to wash your hands of someone else's creation, do your own thing and make changes – lots of changes. As a **Company Doctor** (a person who is sent in to fix sick companies) I had to resist the temptation to throw out my predecessors' management and operations systems and install my own. Sometimes it had to be done but I am not sure that I always made the right decision. The seemingly easy way of starting over is not always the right answer. The other factor is that there is not much bravado in cleaning up someone else's mess because when you get done, it can be looked on as something that was not that bad in the first place, or all you did was tweak it.

Executive management is partly to blame for looking for the silver bullet. Some upper management do not care how the problems are solved, they just want action and results. It has been said that when a country leader is in trouble, his best defense is to declare war on some nearby country. The distraction that results is a total change in priorities and focus. A new ball game is begun. Sometimes people that create change have the similar objectives in mind.

THE IMPACT OF CHANGE

Making changes in an organization is like throwing a rock into a lake. The ripples reach every part of the company. The impact of changes in the organization can be much more profound than most managers imagine. Changes are often made without more than a cursory thought about what these changes will do beyond their planned objectives. Changes often provoke unexpected and unwelcome results in the most unexpected places and situations. Collateral damage can be devastating. Sometimes the changes can cripple or destroy the very functions that are propping up the company.

There are many reasons why change is difficult to achieve. People resist changes because of fear of the unknown (and rightly so). There are many reasons for this, such as fear of loosing out, the ego, preserving ones own turf, etc. An example of fear of the unknown is this story of an Asian company:

WHEN CHANGE SHOULD HAVE SUCCEED

We were transferring complex technology and equipment To a foreign country when one of the shipping crates fell and damaged the delicate machinery inside. A new part had to be made immediately or the program would fall behind schedule. The company had a small machine shop, so we decided to make another part right there. Looking around for metal stock we found a piece of scrap metal about the right size except it had an extension sticking out. We could have cut that off but we were in a hurry and besides, there was room on the machine so it would not interfere with the function. We worked all night turning out the part, and it worked. We stayed on schedule and the technology transfer was successful.

About three years later I revisited the company and while being toured around the production floor, we came upon the machine we had made the emergency repair on, except now there were eight machines because production demands had grown over the past three years. And, there was the part we had hastily made, duplicated in every detail with the extension and all - on all eight machines.

When we asked management, when they duplicated the part, why they didn't cut the extension off. It was oblivious the extension had no function. They replied: "We did not know what the extension was for so we were afraid it would not work properly if we changed it, and we didn't want to let corporate headquarters know we didn't understand."

Here, common sense should have prevailed or, at the very least, they should have questioned the function of the extension. But, they didn't and that was because they feared they would appear less knowledgeable. And, so what would seem to be a simple change to implement was actually a difficult issue and the change process failed.

This and other examples of failed change efforts are proof that the resistance to change is pervasive in most companies. Moreover, the process of making changes is far more complex than might appear to those contemplating the changes. Yet, it is often the giant companies that dabble in bizarre and absurd management experiments, while it is the smaller companies that see these as shortcuts to success or even survival. Even occasional diversions can act like a virus and eat away at the company's vitality. An example was a fast growing company in Culver City.

This company had grown to six hundred or so and was beginning to experience frequent communication problems. The problem was identified as a difficult office arrangement that developed because of rapid growth and little or no facilities planning.

The offices had grown in a haphazard sort of way as the primary company focus had been on engineering and production. There were a lot of small offices and cubicles that the consultant pointed to as obstacles to rapid communications flow.

The plan called for wiping out nearly all of the offices and all of the cubicles so that it was to be nearly all open areas. The theory was that people could access each other more efficiently without offices and cubicles. Access to each other would speed up communications, which would make the company more efficient.

The changes were completed in two months and affected over three hundred people. During that time confusion and resentment were ever present. Confusion because of the greatly increased noise level and the resentment because people lost some of their privacy. Four years later another expansion was required. Another consultant was called in and he recommended that small cubicles be erected, and that the number of conference rooms be increased along with more offices for managers. For those who remembered the office layout before the changes commented that it was both comical and pathetic, the new office layout was a remarkable reconstruction of the old, original layout.

A good example of hidden complexity because of change is the time when an Orange County, California, electronics company decided to change the print numbering system from five digits to nine digits because they were running out of numbers. It was decided to go further and to make the change more effective, adding three Alpha digits to the end of the proposed nine numeric digits. This would allow for classification significance. This was decided because the consultant happened to know one of their competitors used a similar numbering system. The engineering documentation department considered the changes needed in the print system and went ahead without a real effort to understand the consequences. The possibility of problems or issues did come up but they were brushed aside with the, "We will deal with any problem when and if they come up."

The transition period was complex and chaotic. Within days the effects of the change started showing up. The stock room had part bins labeled for five digits; the new system had over twice as many digits so that the full part number would not fit on the same printed line. To get things going, they hand printed all the new numbers until the new cards and labels could be ordered and received. This resulted in many mistakes in reading the part bins. There was software that in finding parts in the system but it could not be modified to fit the new expanded numbering system. A new program had to be written. The entire spare parts system had to be redone because it would only handle five digits. New catalogs had to be developed and ordered to accommodate the new parts system. The attempt to develop a cross reference between the old system and the new required a costly program. Customers had to use two lists to order spares and service was slow, sometimes causing weeks of delay. Later on the cost of the new parts numbering system was determined to be four times the estimate and that did not include the cost of unhappy customers and lost time by employees. What they should have done is develop a dry run to simulate what would happen when the change was made.

Change will affect most every part of the organization, especially areas that are unknown and less visible than the main stream of the company. It is in these less obvious areas that we need to look for the unexpected when we introduce changes.

Change takes time, detailed planning learning, unlearning, and most of all, perseverance. My experience with underestimating change is first hand. After completing a complex new company startup, one that was highly technical, we congratulated ourselves for a successful launch of a major manufacturing company. Now, bolstered with confidence, we faced several small operational changes required because of the country's ethnic diversity and the culture customs. First, I assumed these small changes did not require my close attention because they were, after all, small changes, so I delegated the tasks of planning and follow-up.

Now, that was two mistakes, one after the other. The first mistake is that I failed to realize that there are few simple changes; even small changes can be complex. The second mistake was delegation without my figuring out the details of the changes. The changes were almost defeated because of my ignorance. I had to start over and this time I made sure the planning and execution were impeccable.

LOOKING AROUND FOR SOMETHING TO CHANGE

Like a Boy Scout trying to come up with a good deed for the day

There are examples of *change madness* in troubled companies where groups were organized to go out looking for opportunities to make changes. These groups recommended changes in organizations and procedures that had nothing to do with what really ailed the company. The critical problems were not addressed because everyone was looking in the wrong places. The teams needed to show progress so they changed systems and procedures that promised quick returns. Some changes created new problems they didn't need. The sad part is that real problem solving process was hijacked by the change merchants who promised quick progress and prosperity.

THEY WERE OFF KICKING THE HELL OUT OF MICE WHILE ELEPHANTS WERE WALTZING OUT THE BACK DOOR.

Eventually new management was brought in to restore order. The first thing they did was to put most everything back where it was before the changes took place. Then they began to find out what the real problems were. Eventually they got back on track, but this change experiment cost the company dearly.

MASTERS OF CHANGE

I had the good fortune to watch, first hand, the Singapore Government masterfully orchestratges over several years. The success stories of Singapore are well known, but behind that incredible transformation are stories of praiseworthy management. There were many changes that I watched played out, and to my knowledge they stuck. And, as I watched, the Singapore Government made it look easy. What is so remarkable is that I never saw a change fail, whether it was a low or high profile change or a new program. Some observers might say that the government has the edge over businesses about making changes because all they have to do is legislate the changes. Many of us that have experience with governments know that is far from reality, particularly in the free world. The United States can be used as an example, where someone or some group opposes even the simplest changes and often no mater how beneficial they may promise to be.

What most likely made the Singapore Government so effective was the attention to detail, the planning, and the participation of management from top to bottom. There were big changes and little changes and the ones I was close enough to observe appeared to be managed by several levels of management. The changes I saw happening appeared to be closely orchestrated. The lesson I learned was that management at all levels must be involved, something like a full court press. Extensive delegating was not evident to me. I observed senior members of management out in the thick of things, hands on, helping to affect the changes. At first, I had the feeling that this government was engaged in a little overkill. I soon realized that this was proactive management at its best.

Perhaps the success of the Singapore Government is evident because *they could not afford to fail*. Also, delegation, team autonomy, and empowerment are ideas that have a nice ring to them, and appeal to the theoretical management guru, but to me, did not appear to be their style. Finally, hands on management is, no doubt, the most effective way to get it done.

Some of the current wisdom advocates failure as a process of learning. It is suggested that we need to delegate and empower and let the mistakes begin because the empowered could blossom into an exceptional achiever. We should give the empowered and the delegated degrees of freedom to fail. My comment to that is apparently, these people have never been in a startup where avoiding mistakes, any mistake, is paramount. I would also believe that the Singapore government did not encourage mistakes as a way of developing management skills because the Singapore growth and development was so much like a startup company where everything depends on getting it right the first time.

QUICK FIXES AND OTHER HOKUM

I have been around long enough to see enough new management gimmicks to solve every problem known to man – if only they worked. And yet, I have not seen them all, by any means. There are countless systems, concepts, gimmicks and bazaar disciplines that have invaded the business world that we do not know about because they are born, they may flourish for a short period in some isolated in lesser known enterprises, then they fail and are never heard of again - or until someone rediscovers them and they, like a virus, infect a new generation of unsuspecting companies. The ones we know about are numerous enough and we know about them because they are doing or have done considerable.

ENABLING CHANGE

It is not enough to justify change because even when that is the correct call, you still have the problem of enabling the required change. Few environments are receptive to change; you could say many are actually hostile to change. When you throw a change into an environment that is not ready or susceptible to that particular change, you are asking for failure. Along with environments that are not ready, we have those companies that are not capable of dealing with change. Some are so fragile that even simple changes can be destructive. It can come down to: "How much change can you stand?"

An example is a company in the Northwest who made computer peripherals. They had been successful early on but now that Japanese competition had entered the market, they could not compete in quality, reliability and cost.

I was hired to help prepare a plan to build another manufacturing facility in Southeast Asia and the project was on the front burner. Management had made up their minds that the solution was to change the manufacturing base and move it half way around the world. They believed a lower manufacturing cost would revitalize the company.

For the next two weeks I interviewed every executive and manager in the company. I also went through hundreds of files and reports on everything from quality reports, customer complaints, market share history, employee turnover, exit interviews and much more. The conclusion I reached was that the problem was not just the cost of their manufacturing base but the quality of their management. The problems were late product introduction, poor quality, poor reliability, inefficient manufacturing systems and more. I was convinced that moving would not solve their immediate problems but would only exacerbate them, and these problems would follow them wherever they went.

Now I had a problem. Management was convinced they needed change and it would be difficult to convince them that *they* were the problem. In addition, the company was both financially weak as well as very thin in the new product development. This magnitude of change could derail or overshadow efforts that were more of a survival nature.

There is only so much creativity and problem solving energy in any one company. The decisions as to what to concentrate on are critical. However, it is most often needs to be survival first and improvement second. This company did not comprehend the complexity and cost of starting up a manufacturing company half way around the world. The fact was that they did not fully appreciate how much trouble they were in right here at home. My report and recommendations were that a change as complicated and costly as setting up an offshore manufacturing operation should not be contemplated at this time. Above all other efforts, getting your priorities right is the highest priority. But, the most troubling factor was that this move would not solve one of their problems. They did not need change; they needed to *get it right.* All the problems they had would follow them anywhere they went and it is a certainty that they would pick up more problems along the way. Setting up a subsidiary or division half way around the world will result in complications with a capital "C".

I developed a plan to address the problems on a broad, frontal effort, which included strengthening senior management.

The plan also included a small task force to address each problem and a full court press on customer satisfaction. My conclusions were presented to an unresponsive executive staff that would not be denied their change. One of the executives drove me to the airport that afternoon and he remarked that I acted like a man who didn't care from where his next paycheck was coming. My answer was: "Yes, if it meant I had to help a company do serious damage to itself."

The company went ahead with the manufacturing base change and was unsuccessful in regaining market share and reducing cost, partly because of the high offshore startup costs. Just fourteen months later the company was sold at a bargain-basement price. The most notable omission was the failure to address the survival issues.

The most important part of this story is that although a lower cost manufacturing base might bring long term lower cost, the priority to recapture market share and customer confidence was essential. Changes were immaterial when faced with more fundamental and urgent problems. It maters little if you were to achieve lower cost two years form now if your environment could not tolerate a disruptive change in the near term. This was another case of misplaced priorities and working on the wrong problem at the wrong time.

IT'S A WAR

So far all I have talked about is how bad change can be for your company, especially if your company really needs to get it right. So, let's look at the other side of change (and there is always another side). If you have really considered all the available aspects of change and you are still convinced you need to do it, here are some pointers on how to make it work.

If you are planning a metamorphic type of change, you need to take an aggressive approach that will closely resemble an offensive campaign. You need to start thinking that you are pitted against adversaries who will defeat your plans for improvement and future success unless you treat your offensive as a well planned and detailed assault. My way is not the only way, but it has worked for me. What I have developed is a set of guidelines and flexible rules that can be changed or modified as needed but they are the core of my strategy.

RULE 1

The change process is usually organized under Project Management direction. Teams and other empowered or autonomous management styles are not appropriate if you wish to achieve swift success.

RULE 2

Choose the best project manager and members the company has to offer. Insist on having the best even if you are accused of overkill. If there are some skills and experiences that are important to the project that are not available in the company, go outside.

In a few companies, I have been offered people that came to me with lavish praise from their management, only to find that they were problem people and management did not know what to the with them. The real performers were hidden from me. The sad truth is that management wanted change but was not prepared to give it their best.

RULE 3

Defeat the old system or old order of things as quickly as possible. Do not let the resisters pretend to embrace the new change while they secretly rely on the old. Cortez destroyed his ships when he arrived in the new world. His men were highly motivated to conquer the new world because with no boats to return home, they had to succeed. That strategy is well advised here, although it also goes without saying, your change had better be right.

RULE 4

Energize your team by making them special. Give them an identity that sets them apart from the day-to-day activities. I like my people to feel like they can do the next to the impossible. Starting from the beginning we operate on our own clock and we take no prisoners – whatever it takes to succeed. In some situations I began my staff meetings at 6:00 AM when the rest of the company is eight to five. My thirty-minute staff meetings end sharply at 6:30 AM. Then, the Staff meeting reviews the results of the status meeting and we are on our feet at 7:00 AM. We are prepared to go the extra ten miles. Failure is unthinkable. That, however, is just one of many ways to energize the project members. In the beginning there are a few members that quietly object to things like an early schedule and long work day, but very soon it becomes part of what makes us different and unstoppable.

RULE 5

Isolate the project group as much as possible. I often find a separate building to house the project group. This is important because you need a degree of isolation in order to avoid distractions and the critics who do not want the change to succeed.

RULE 6

If the company's standard procedures threaten the project, you must find a way to go over, under, around or through whatever is in your way.

An example was a large company that had a long procurement cycle. It had such a backlog that a procurement request would not be acted upon for at least ten days; this was unacceptable for our project. We were retooling the entire product line and we had to order thousands of parts. In addition our project was the setting up of a large manufacturing subsidiary in a foreign country. Everything was on a tight schedule. The excessive procurement lead-time would have made it impossible to meet the fast-track schedule.

I convinced management to allow us to set up our own project procurement operation inside our own project team. Procurement requests were acted upon in twenty fours hours. The project stayed on schedule. Incidentally, the company was forced to look at their long lead-time procurement practices and origination. A complete overhaul was done and in six months the cycle had been trimmed down to 48-hour cycle.

Resistance to going around obstacles is to be expected. However, I have never been denied a temporary standard procedure deviation when the request was properly presented to the management. The simple truth is, if you fail, it doesn't mater why your project failed. All that matters is that you failed.

RULE 7

Make sure that your project group is loyal, motivated and believes in the mission. One cynical or insincere person can destroy your project. Constructive debate and people that challenge are not the problem. However, cynical people will spread their poison to others. Of all the personality defects we deal with, cynicism is the most dangerous.

RULE 8

Take the time to encourage the group as a group and as individuals. Change projects do not always run smoothly, you can help to make the rough parts less discouraging by working with your people when they need you. A project leader is not only a leader; he is a father confessor, a teacher, a disciplinarian mentor, a coach and above all someone the people respect.

RULE 9

Develop a master plan and detailed tracking system. I often track as many as 300 to 500 items every day. We can status the entire project in thirty minutes. There is no excuse for not knowing the status of every detail of your project, at anytime, so that you can track, assess, adjust and apply resources and support where it is most needed.

There are planning programs that are almost ubiquitous across the business landscape. It is the generation of useless planning charts, tracking devices and progress reports that bear no resemblance to what has happened or is happening and what might be predicted. These devices are generated to convince someone, your customers, your boss, or the management that everything is under control. Most of these are out of date before they are half finished.

A familiar sight is management giving a tour to a customer who is shown a very impressive control type chart that covers half the wall of the conference room, and whose detail is impressive. In most cases management is aware that the chart is not accurate, but no one will actually challenge such an impressive display.

These progress-reporting devices are not usually generated to deceive anyone, but they are often meant to impress. Serious people do use these devices and they do work if all the rules are followed.

Charts and such are popular because management believes that professional management devices like these bring greater control and visibility (and it doesn't hurt the ol' image either), and they are sometimes meant to impress customers and investors who are looking over their shoulders. It would not be so bad if most of these chart zealots knew how to use them. Some of the control charts are so complicated that it takes someone with considerable experience and insight to be able to read them.

A more common shortcoming is that these charts are not always kept up to date. They can become quickly out of date. Not only do they become misleading, they foster contempt because most people know they don't depict the real status. These poorly maintained control devices also mislead some people into believing that they are actually in control and were the truth known, some sort of remedial or corrective action could have been possible.

RULE 10

Prepare frequent and detailed progress reports that show the good and the not so good and what your group is doing about it. Do it up right with a quality presentation that leaves the audience well informed and impressed. If possible, let your group be part of the presentations. It is not only good experience for them but also gives them exposure and an identity. Do not embellish your work or in any way mislead your audience. Your credibility is one of your most important assets. Support for your project is essential and it comes because management believes and respects you and your group – keep it that way.

RULE 11

Treat your enemies and detractors gently unless they really threaten the project. Make it easy for them to join in the winners' circle when the dust has settled and the project is a recognized success. A successful program can win over 70% of the company. The other 30% will just have to live with it.

RULE 12

Keep your project together long enough to know the project will not unravel when your group is dismantled. Plan your downsizing and departure as well as how you designed the project. It would be gravely unfortunate for the project to come apart because you didn't finish the job.

RULE 13

Make sure that you reward your project members as a group and individually. Go out of your way to insure that the company recognizes their efforts and their achievements. There should be both accolades and material rewards such as monetary gains and promotions where deserved. Modesty is not appropriate here. This is not just for the project members; it is also for the future projects that will benefit from your example and the show of gratitude by the company.

RULE 14

Before you depart or go on to another project, arrange a recap of the entire project with the highest management level you can reach. Show the accomplishments and the things that could have been done better. Some people might think that this is the time for a sales job and an opportunity to solicit accolades and praise. Actually, it is a time to set the record straight. You and your group know what really happened but others may not know what really transpired. A great deal respect will be the reward for strait talk, simply stated, and with a dash of brevity.

Change is inevitable; everything is changing, even the cosmos. But, in the pragmatic world of business, change has to be anticipated and controlled. Companies can literally destroy themselves because of the idea that new is better and sweeter, and change is the answer to their problems. Change can beguile, deceive and betray us. Change has no master.

Chapter XI

BOARD OF DIRECTORS

Where mice kicking begins

THE BUCK STOPS SOMEWHERE - RIGHT?

Even CEO's and Presidents have bosses. In corporations, it is the Board of Directors who have the ultimate authority and responsibility. They are the high priesthood of enterprise wisdom and corporate governance. They have the license to do anything, legal that is, to insure the well being of the corporation. Their job is to look after the welfare of the enterprise for the investors, a task not all board of directors do well.

The board has the ultimate responsibility and authority, but often acts like it has neither. Sometimes late to act, or frequently usurping management authority and prerogatives:

They are often indifferent and aloof until disaster strikes. It is an enigma, but still, it is part of a system that is the best legal contrivance to promote investment the world has ever known.

It is hard to imagine any other system that could have encouraged and supported so much investment from every part of the world. Still, there are so many ways it can be misused that one wonders if the laws and rules for boards of corporate governess are strong enough to insure the investor will get first-rate and legal management of their investment.

Corporate Governance, the Board of Directors prime responsibility, is a special responsibility that requires the overall surveillance, long range planning and constant vigilance over the corporation. Yet, there are many examples of disaster striking and the Board of Directors didn't have a clue it was coming. That implies they were either asleep at the switch, preoccupied with less important issues, incompetent or perhaps a little bit of all three.

WHO IS RUNNING THE SHOW ANYWAY?

In my opinion, the most efficient management structure is a fully autocratic one with one person at the helm. That sounds a little undemocratic, but not really when you consider that most companies are, in fact, operating that way. The CEO or president is that single authority who is the driving force in most intuitions. But, even he has a boss – the Board of Directors. Still, there are unbalanced management realities that allow grievous mistakes, omissions and illegal activities.

An example of this imbalance is when we have successful companies that, by the CEO or presidents sheer strength (or the weakness of the board of directors), he or she can operate without constraints, controls or piercing accountability. This can go on through thick and thin, and sometimes only when the company becomes desperate, or actually fails, does the board come to grips with their responsibility.

When a company is successful it is usually due to the sheer force of the chief operations officer. In some cases, this success comes only after having dragged the board of directors kicking and screaming into a victorious event or campaign. Such an event is likely to leave the board even less assertive and less apt to question what is really going on.

A MUST DO LIST FOR THE BOARD OF DIRECTORS

So, if the most efficient mode is to the let the chief executive have his head, then just what is the most effective mode of operation for the board? My abbreviated version is:

The board is there to ensure the company is managed by the best executive staff that the company can field starting with the best CEO or president they can find.

It is there to give direct and indirect support the efforts of the executive management being mindful not to interfere, or take over functions and responsibilities classically belonging to management. That is unless there is emanate danger that management can not or will not act to resolve.

Develop a strategy and course of action, and it is there to help the executive management explore and to make course adjustments and be a constant reminder to stay the course, or change it as conditions indicate.

It is there to assertively monitor the progress, or lack there of, and in this regard must remain vigilant at all times. This does not mean superficial reviews. It means stripping away all the dressing, façade, and appearances so that the real state of the institution is understood by all concerned.

It means establishing a review policy of no frills, no salesmanship, and a two-sided exposure that says it, the way it is – good and bad. This means, accurate, if not brutal, numbers crunching and real debate as to progress and or the lack of it. The board must also understand the rules by which the numbers are acquired. This is essential, because just about anything can be presented favorably if you are in control of rules by which the information is acquired and assembled. This also means tenacious attention to detail by all of the board members - something that is not too often the case. They are often more comfortable with the big picture and they often prefer to leave the details to the operations management. This can be dangerous. There is no one else that can challenge the method that produced the assembled data. Some learned experts advise that boards should operate on a different level than operations, a broader and loftier purview. This is most likely the preferred board's modus operandi. But, it can be flawed, depending on the circumstances, and the people involved. It is essential that the details be examined, at least sampled by the board from time to time. What is even more essential is that the board understands how the details were acquired and prepared because bad happenings and a foreboding future can be easily disguised by a clever professional. It is there to replace, or reinforce executive management when they deem it necessary. Too often they wait until the company is desperate before they act.

It is there to help evolve and approve major strategy and mission changes.

It has the responsibility to ensure that financial scrutiny is squeaky clean and that can mean the direct hiring of outside audit functions that report directly to the Board of Directors.

It is there to ensure the corporation is legal in all respects wherever it is involved.

It comes down to this: The Board of Directors must ensure that the enterprise is legal in all respects, in whatever country jurisdiction or environment it resides, or functions, and that the investor's interest along with the general welfare of the employees is paramount at all times. Transparency is a difficult culture to maintain but in the long run it is essential to ensure the overall success of the enterprise.

WHAT DO DIRECTORS DO?

The Board of Director's most effective position is to approve the executive management's missions, approving new strategy while staying in the background until it must affect a major change - before disaster strikes. The board must ensure that a balance of management elements, including both financial and moral responsibilities is in force for the overall long term good of the corporation.

IT'S THE DETAILS STUPID, NOT JUST THE BIG PICTURE

The most common weakness of many Boards of Directors seems to be a lack of periodic, in-depth review that gets down to the detail and how the detail is acquired. In the many corporations it is the executive arm that hires the auditors. This is like having the rabbits watch the lettuce. It needs to define the rules that the company will function with and then make sure the rules are being followed.

There is a mistaken concept that the board's job is there to oversee what is going on and should not have to look at the details. Or as often happens, the reviews become a standard format that is prepared and delivered by the executive group. These reviews can become a habit and cover just the issues and depth that is convenient for the executive staff. This can go on for years or until disaster strikes and then it becomes obvious that there were deeper issues and subjects that were not touched all that time.

Board meetings and reviews should be specific enough to reveal serious problems before they become fully developed. There should be no walking on eggs when it comes to laying open the pertinent and vital details. Not only should numbers be questioned, but the rules by which the numbers are acquired should be understood and agreed upon. The problem is that, not too unlike mortal men, boards of directors develop habits of working on things they like to work on, the big picture, and they often avoid working on things they dislike, like boring detail or exploring the premises upon which data and the status is based.

THEY COME IN MANY COLORS

From another point of view, the Board of Directors is a bad idea made worse by members who serve there own interest before the investor.

> Power hungry directors
> Fearful and over-reactive, cover-their-rear type directors
> Too many inside directors
> Too many professional directors serving on too many other boards
> A stagnant board with little or no new blood
> A board infested with director cliques with self-serving agendas

A board with total worship of increasing the return on investment (ROI) at the expense of everything, including employees, legalities, and other moral considerations.

THE PREDILECTION OF DIRECTORS

Directors come predisposed and with strong preferences because of their vast experiences. That is why they are chosen to sit on the board. That background is essential for the process of enlightened governance. But sometimes the board is composed with members that are there to support their spongers interest. Money lenders and major investors often insist they have one or more of theirs on the board to observe and warn them of impending danger. Sometimes they are there for more sinister reasons, like finding out the companies vulnerability for possible take-over action. The more outside directors with their own agendas, the less efficient and the more controversy will occupy the boardroom.

The question is: Do we need a board of directors? The answer is yes; the law says we do if you want to be a corporation. The second question is how should the board of directors do their job? They should ensure that the management is doing their job, and not try to do it for them or wait until a disaster in upon them before they act. But what can we expect unless we know what kind of director we are depending on?

TYPES OF DIRECTORS

There are many types of directors. We could come up with a long list of types but the ones I find interesting are these:

I WANT MY OWN SANDBOX MEMBER

What is wrong with some board of directors? Some members have a problem with being in a tangential capacity. Most directors have considerable on-hands experience with management and can relate to the issues and problems. For some directors it is difficult to leave their personal ambitions and habit formed management experiences behind. Sitting on a board of directors once a month or every three months is not like having a real position of line responsibility. The problem is: *These people do not have their own sandbox to play in.*

For some, sitting on the board, watching at a distance, the action they grew up with is just too much – they have to tamper. Some plot their own future in the CEO's or other executive position. These people are not objective, and will, if not curbed, bring down the current management, that can bring division and disunity to a company.

THE DO NOTHING DIRECTORS

And then, there are others that do not do much at all. They just attend the meetings and ride the current wave of popular opinion, and take no constructive position or direction if it is not where the rest of the board is going.

THE CELEBRITY BOARD MEMBER

This is the type of board that has a host of impressive names on their roster. These members are who's who in their fields and have been assembled to impress some aspect of the company's interest like bankers, investors, customers, political contacts, and people with key customers. So many of these people love to have it known that they sit on many (the more the better) boards of directors. They are almost always recognized as powerful and successful business people. You see much more of this in developing countries where a person's image is very important in the tight business circles in which they live. Sitting on ten or more boards is not unusual.

PRINCIPLE INVESTOR - WATCHDOG MEMBER

This is a member who is on the board to watch how the money he or she represents is being spent. They are especially watchful of decisions and trends that may go against the investors' agendas. Sometimes these people are helpful but may not know a great deal about operations and how to navigate the rocky shoals of management. There are several notable differences between Private, Bank, and Venture Capitalist investors, but basically they are driven by the same merciless master - Return on Investment (ROI). A little of this kind of board membership goes a long way, but it may be necessary to keep the capital flowing in.

THE PRAYING MANTIS MEMBER

This guy is not content with the role of a board member and yearns for the action of being in the thick of things. He wants the top job, president or CEO, but has to bide his time and wait for the right openings. Criticism is carefully hidden behind innuendoes and vague comparisons with his own successes (real or enhanced) Like, "the way we handled that problem was . . ." He may plan a systematic exposure of the weakness of the present management. He must, however, keep his agenda secret and position himself for the time when his fellow members ask him to take over. If asked, his acceptance will be carefully rehearsed with surprise and humility, however, he will accept.

THE TECHNICAL GURU MEMBER

Usually, this person is a principle in the company, perhaps a co-founder or the inventor who was an original member of the board of directors. Most of the time he can't wait to get back to his work and out of the boardroom. He is usually tactless and blunt when it comes to the games board members play. That may not endear him to some of his fellow board members who often end up restructuring the board to his exclusion. The loss of the Technical Guru at the board level can be serious or even fatal when the company is in the leading technology business. Particularly early in a company's beginnings, technical representation at the board level can be critical for the board to understand the progress of the product development, the technical problems, and the technical options available. His vision may be one of the critical anchors the company has.

THE PROFESSIONAL BOARD MEMBER

This type of board member can be a great help to a company if he or she is really interested in being more than an observer even if there is not a strong background in the company's business. The problem is that this type is often sitting on other boards and may not be able to give his best for any one company. Some of these directors belong to ten or more Boards of Directors and my sport several chairmanships. It can be an ego thing but it is doubtful they can really contribute to but a few boards. The dichotomy is that these people have the experience to help companies and could mentor junior board members. However, it is not likely because these people are spread very thin.

THE TENDERFOOT DIRECTOR

This is the first time director, usually an inside executive. Too few companies practice an apprentice program for this poor, lost soul, but it is needed and could be the most important step in the director's development and success.

I remember the first time I was nominated to a board of directors; boy was I green and nervous. I just sat there trying to look knowledgeable while keeping my mouth shut until (and I dreaded it would happen) someone asked me for my opinion. I did not make a great impression, but over time you find your way by observing and making assumptions – that are sometimes wrong. In my opinion it is a terrible process but it could be made better if a senior board member would be assigned to mentor a tenderfoot. Better yet, our corporations would greatly benefit if perspective board members were required to take a college level course in corporate governance.

THE INSIDE BOARD MEMBER EXECUTIVE BOARD MEMBER

Usually this is a co-founder or a key management type executive that brings reality and urgency to the rest of the board members. This is an *inside* board member and is usually the CEO and or one or more of vice presidents and often the chief financial officer. The roll of the insider can be important as it usually reflects on programs, issues, problems and proposals that are closely associated with the operations side of the corporation. There are many who are fearful of too many inside board members. I don't see the problem with inside directors unless there is a need for diversity because of the nature of the companies business.

Insiders are not always popular with the outsiders because of conflicting agendas and the best way to achieve them. However, some companies have learned to use the expertise of both insiders and outsiders in selective operations assignments to make the board of directors a really effective force. From the operations view this is called, "putting your board to work," which is a good trick if you can make it happen. In more recent years some boards have become more and more involved in what the operations management is doing. That can be good or bad depending on how it is done, and what the motives are.

THE CHAIRMAN OF THE BOARD

The top of the pyramid, king of the hill, the top of the pile, leader of leaders, where the buck stops, the end of the management rainbow . . . Right, but not always. It may be that but it is most likely just another job. One would think the Chairman would be the leader, but this is not always the case. Often the chairman is there because he or she owns, or represents a large block of shares in the company and may be happy to sit back and let someone else drive the hard issues. How the Chairman of the board, defines the job, and does the job is a many-splintered thing. The modes operandi of a board chairman is as varied as life in the sea. It can be as disconnected and uninvolved as taking roll and reading the minutes to making every decision including some that classically belong to operations.

I would suggest that the chairman's roll should be no less assertive and involved as the CEO or president and that he or she be totally aware of the company's health. Most of all, I expect the Chairmen to be a relentless driver of the board members. I expect him to set the corporation agenda and be the example of intense interest and proactive involvement in guiding the board.

WHO IS TO BLAME FOR SOARING EXECUTIVE COMPENSATION?

Guess who, the Board of Directors. Some people blame the compensation committees, but they are a committee - right? When boards approve colossal pay-packages that is a danger signal that too many board members are beholden to a major force that is really in charge and they fear that person more than the investors.

WITHOUT A LICENSE, HOW DO YOU KNOW THEY CAN DRIVE?

What would be supremely helpful would be a primer of the duties and the legal responsibilities of a director that include the moral considerations as well. The possibility that a young director candidate would be a much better asset and influence if he or she was educated in the directors lore is too great to ignore. Boards of directors would do well to add such a requirement to their charter.

Much of the problem with ineffective or illegal board activity can be because of a novice or ill trained board member. Some never really understand their job and over time become immune to their own growing ineffectiveness. When a CEO or President is grossly incompetent or engaged in illegal activity, the Chairman and the board should be indicted right along with him.

I firmly believe that the corporation failures should be laid at the door of the Chairman and the board of directors who, too often, hide behind the chief operating officer with the lame excuse, "We didn't know." "They didn't know" is no defense. It is their job to know.

A final thought: Both the executive management, members and the board of directors can have a serious conflict of interest because of their, often considerable, ownership in the company. Decisions that affect the long-term value of the company can be sacrificed for short-term higher stock value and therefore their own stock options value. The temptation to become rich over night is just too great for some. Decisions that would favor long term growth and prosperity are often put aside. The only real control over this type of greed is the majority of the stockholders that are hopefully led by a honest, fearless chairman.

Assuming the chairman is a part of the problem there is only one last resort, **a stockholders revolt.**

The End